C000177084

'This book is a must-read for any [...] of intimacy and intentionality in [...] with such honesty, wisdom and [...] into spiritual principles and bibli[...] [...]ights, you know you are reading words from a woman who has done plenty of walking to back up her talking. There are profound and significant insights to be found within these pages – I cannot recommend *Face to Face* highly enough.'

Cathy Madavan, speaker, writer, coach and author

'Jen Baker is the real deal! She has an amazing ability to draw you in with her story. As she describes her journey to freedom you will be inspired to walk out your own journey to health and wholeness. Leading in faith and not shrinking back in fear is her mantra. She is one of the best at identifying the gaps and bringing answers.

'So many believers struggle with the fact that they are saved and yet not living free. Jen is able to bring you forward, with her insight into Scripture, brilliance in application, and adding a bit of humour to boot.

'My favourite quote: "Purpose is not a destination you arrive at; it is a journey you live out." (Mic-drop!) You can be sure to experience a shift in your perspective, and will be transformed in your heart and mind as you read it!'

Karen Hagan, North Central University, international speaker, mentor and writer

'Using Moses' journey as a metaphor for our own lives and sprinkled with stories of her own, Jen gently challenges us to discard the baggage that prevents us from knowing God intimately and calls us to a life of faith and trust. With her delightful conversational style, Jen tackles one of the most important areas for our Christian walk. A great devotional read!'

Tania Harris, pastor, speaker, author and founder of God Conversations

'Grace was planned before time began. I'm struck by the immensity of the revelation Jen explores. God desires to bring us from hiding to holiness, from sinners saved by grace to empowered saints, from removed by distance to face to face. Jen Baker paints this truth, artfully displayed in the beautiful colours of God's grace. *Face to Face* is an eternal game-changer for every believer.'

Dawn Scott Damon, pastor, author and national speaker

'Prophetic, practical and beautiful! Jen Baker's book, *Face to Face* is a beautiful, prophetic call from the heavenly Father for intimacy. Jen draws you into this life-changing message with her own real-life stories. She is extremely practical in helping overcome obstacles with clarity on "next steps" to take for the reader. It has the potential to help every believer go deeper in their relationship with God.'

Steve Uppal, All Nations Church

'This inspiring work is filled with Scriptures and thoughts that warm the heart, raise the soul, and impulse the will to lead a godly life preparing each of us to best meet the Lord face to face!'

Gary Hill, President HELPS ministries Inc. Editor in chief, The Discovery Bible

'*Face to Face* is a beautifully written and wonderfully transparent book. Knowing Jen Baker as I do, I can see how what she's written so completely encapsulates the beauty of her relationship with God. To quote her words, "the desert is where we often meet our destiny", is to understand the way in which she has grappled with the pains and pressures of life without losing her hope in Christ and her love for his people.

'Jen's writing enables her readers to see beyond God, the wish-granter, and into the truths of an empowering relationship with him where maturity and love replace the confusion that happens when everything doesn't work out how we planned. She takes us from the place in which "hiding becomes part of humanity" to the full-on, open-faced, joyous communion of being changed from glory to glory, piece by piece, into his image.

'Jen brings such clarity of insight to the way in which love, trust and vulnerability with God creates its own holy place – the cleft in the rock – in which every Christian can be hidden from the brokenness of the world. She shows how the believer can be protected and kept safe from anything the world or the enemy could attempt to derail us with. It's all about relationship, with God first and out from there into our worlds. This is such a beautiful book and so full of godly wisdom and insight.'

Bev Murrill, Kyria Network, bevmurrill.com

'Practical and spiritual applications abound in this book from Jen Baker. Jen lays out her story of trial and triumph. Confronting her fears and coming face to face with her source in Christ, Jen exposes the hidden life of her past and shares some life-changing truths and principles regarding life's hidden battles.

'*Face to Face* will cause life-changing victories in Christ and testify to those going through similar experience and travail. A must read.'

Shaneen Clarke, international speaker and author

'How can we see God face to face? Jen Baker looks to the story of Moses, and how he, with all of his faults and foibles, was led into the presence of God and became a world changer. With deep vulnerability, Jen shares stories of how she too encounters the living Lord. You'll find her a trustworthy and inspiring guide, one who models radical faith.'

Amy Boucher Pye, speaker and author

'Jen has written a manifesto for our time. No one needs convincing that these days are full of division and segregation (despite our many attempts at connection). Jen reminds us, with beautiful storytelling and provocative, scriptural exposition that it doesn't have to be this way. She evokes the dream of Eden, like a memory that was lost and offers a tangible invitation to remember. If there is a stirring for something more within you, it's time to turn these pages and discover the truth; there is a better story, a truer humanity, a yearning within us all, to be face to face with God, once again.'

Joshua Luke Smith, poet, preacher, producer,
joshualukesmith.com

FACE
to
FACE

Life lessons from Moses
– exploring intimacy with God

Jen Baker

Authentic

First published 2019 by Authentic Media Limited,
PO Box 6326, Bletchley, Milton Keynes, MK1 9GG.
authenticmedia.co.uk

British Library Cataloguing in Publication Data
A catalogue record for this book is available from the British Library.
ISBN: 978-1-78893-056-7
978-1-78893-057-4 (e-book)

Cover design by Mercedes Piñera
Printed and bound by CPI Group (UK) Ltd., Croydon, CR0 4YY

There is only one who deserves this dedication – the one who pursued me from the beginning of time, who sat with me in my darkest hours, who calls out my truest purpose and who ceaselessly fills my deepest desires:

Jesus.

Contents

Acknowledgments

I ran the London Marathon in 2012 and one of the greatest lessons I learned is this: it is not possible to finish a race without a team. I'll be forever grateful to my team (Sarah, Brian and Chrissy) who helped me cross the finish line outside Buckingham Palace.

In similar fashion, and for more than any other book I've written, this journey has felt as if I was running a marathon. While I spent hundreds of hours writing in solitude, there are numerous people who have metaphorically run the race with me over many months.

Always, first and foremost are my parents – Bob and Barb Baker. They are my greatest supporters; more than anyone on earth, they have shaped and moulded me by their unwavering support over the years. As a lover of words, I still have no vocabulary to describe my deep love for and gratitude to them. I love you, Mom and Dad . . . so much.

My immediate family who cheer me on from across the Atlantic – thank you.

Bobby and Kimi, thank you for allowing me to share about precious (and precocious) Dorothy, who will no doubt be President one day.

Harry Rudge, thank you for letting me include a story about you as a 3-year-old, even though you are now a very cool 15-year-old.

The members of my prayer team who bring me before the throne room, continually fighting battles when I am too weary to fight – thank you.

Lisa – you know this would never have been finished in time without your help! *Thank you* for the copious (daily) cappuccinos you delivered to keep me going, prayers in the ridiculously early hours of the morning, and the hundreds of other details you took care of (and still do) for me on a regular basis to keep the ministry running smoothly. You are both a servant of the Lord and a force to be reckoned with in the kingdom, and I honour you.

Ali – I am truly blessed to have you in my life (even though I've never met you!) and I thank you from the bottom of my heart for all your encouragement, support and countless prayers. Knowing I could text you at any time to pray was a tremendous blessing; you epitomize the word 'faithful'.

Georgia – my 'rent-a-friend' – you have been the most fabulous passenger along this journey and I thank you for encouraging me and making me laugh in the hard times. I love you!

My UK family and also Bath City Church, my church family – there are too many of you to name, but please know how much you have encouraged me, cheered me on and blessed me by your interest in this journey. Thank you for asking how it was going and encouraging me not to quit on those difficult days!

Authentic Media – we did it again! Donna, Becky, Charlie and the entire team: *thank you* for being so encouraging, understanding, patient when the manuscript was late(!), supportive and helpful from beginning to end. You make it a much more enjoyable process and I appreciate you so much!

Mollie Barker – thank you once again for making me sound better than I am! Your attention to detail, professionalism, kindness and wordsmith abilities are a true blessing.

Finally, to the reader – thank you for allowing me to step into your world once again with my words, thoughts, prayers and belief in you and in all God has for your future. You are a gift to this world and I am cheering you on to all God has for you now and in your future. The best is truly yet to come.

Introduction

*We are able to have as much of God as we want.
Christ puts the key to His treasure chest in our
hands and invites us to take all we desire. If
someone is allowed into a bank vault, told to
help himself to the money, and leaves without one
cent, whose fault is it if he remains poor? And
whose fault is it that Christians usually have such
meager portions of the free riches of God?*

Alexander Maclaren[1]

God has a wonderful sense of humour.

Many years ago, while in-between speaking sessions at a women's conference, I chose to take a walk with Jesus in the nearby woods.

As we meandered along the path, I would slightly close my fist – imagining my earthly hand lovingly held by a nail-pierced hand – the two of us enjoying the trail together, gently swinging arms as we went. Soon we came upon a fairly large mud puddle in the middle of the pathway. Without thinking, I began walking around the puddle while 'holding on to' Jesus' hand. Halfway around the puddle I looked down; realizing I hadn't moved over far enough and that Jesus was 'standing' in the puddle, I laughed and said, '*Oops* – sorry, Jesus, you're in the mud puddle!'

Without skipping a beat I immediately heard in my spirit: 'Jen, I've walked on water before.'

Gulp.

Put in my place, I relaxed at his sense of humour and carried on, revelling in the reality that God loves an invitation to our everyday moments.

An invitation that, at one time, was not necessary.

***

All of creation beheld the first dance of oneness between the Father and humanity, sensing profound vulnerability, without any anxiety. Man and woman, humanity and the Godhead, naked and unashamed; equally sated in laughter and content in silence; experiencing complete transparency and unadulterated pleasure, together as one.

As unconditionally loved children, Adam and Eve walked in the cool of the garden, blissfully unaware of an enemy lingering nearby, waiting for an opportune time to sow division, destruction and death into their paradisal home.

Finally the moment came, and on the heels of one fateful decision, hiding and shame entered the garden – hitching a ride on the heart of humanity, creating a chasm fit for a cross. Thankfully, through the blood of Jesus Christ, we have been redeemed to relationship – creating a way to approach the throne of grace with boldness (Heb. 4:16). But shame is not easily uprooted and will declare ownership where none exists. Therefore, for many people, the thought of approaching holiness invokes great hesitation and sure trepidation – preferring mystery to proximity.

One man well acquainted with hiding was Moses; he was literally hidden *from birth*. Not only that – after murdering a man he went into hiding again, and then at the appearance of

God in a burning bush Moses 'hid his face'. Hiding was synonymous with Moses for the first half of his life . . . yet, as we will see, our beginning does not determine our ending.

Several years ago, while sitting in my lounge doing devotions, I noticed that in Exodus 3 'Moses hid his face' and in Exodus 33 he spoke with God 'face to face'. I began to wonder: how does one go from hiddenness to holiness?

Moses will be our tour guide on this journey, as we observe the steps he took to leave a life of hiding once and for all. If you are tired of hiding from God, hiding from others – perhaps even hiding from yourself – allow Moses' story to become *your* story.

Hiding began in the Garden of Eden, so our journey will begin by exploring the original relationship with God and humanity: a relational bond of perfect intimacy that was shattered by an insidious enemy.

Next, we will consider what caused Moses to cease hiding and to start trusting – discovering that our greatest safety is often found in facing our deepest fears.

Finally, we will remind ourselves of a future reality: when all of God's children experience his glory as it was at creation. We will anticipate this destined union; the deepest expression of love as the Bride and her Bridegroom become one – an unexplainable manifestation of God's holiness in humanity, no more pain and no more tears, only perfect harmony and irrepressible joy.

United again – face to face, naked and unashamed.

Part One

In the Beginning

1

The Garden

But the LORD God called to the man, 'Where are you?'

Gen. 3:9

It began – and ended – with a phone call.

I knew my friend had been in counselling for trauma she endured in her childhood, and on an especially difficult day she phoned me to listen and cry with her. I rushed over, listened, prayed, cried, comforted and then drove home. By the time I pulled into my driveway I was trembling all over and felt an unsettled, nauseous feeling in the pit of my stomach. I ran into my flat,[1] threw myself into a corner, curled up into a ball, rocked back and forth, and mumbled, 'What is happening to me?' In the face of my fear, God suddenly felt non-existent, or at the very least non-communicative. Though I had no previous recollection before this, somehow I knew: I also had been abused.

We all have experienced our 'perfect world' becoming shattered in a moment. Perhaps it's that age when you finally see your parents as humans, not heroes, or arriving home to a note from your spouse saying they cannot do this any more. It could be a child who confesses to an addiction or lifestyle choice that you don't agree with, or a financial crisis created by an invest-ment or business deal gone wrong. One minute everything seems to be moving at an acceptable pace and all seems right with the world, and the next we are finding it hard to trust even those who are most trustworthy in our lives.

I wonder if Adam and Eve felt similar feelings on that fateful day when the serpent tempted them and the children traded their perfect world for a harsh reality of life separated from per-fect love – slamming the door of innocence behind them after one bite of forbidden fruit.

Coming to terms with the fact that I had been abused (by a babysitter when I was 6 years old) felt like a door slam-ming in the face of my innocence, and I spent the next few weeks in denial, willing it to be opened once again. But once slammed, it cannot reopen – at least, that is what I believed at the time.

We will revisit this later, but let me finish with another phone call.

It took place a few years after the visit to my friend and this time I was the one doing the calling – confronting the babysit-ter for what he had done to me as a child. There isn't space, or purpose, to divulge much detail, but over the phone and with much fear and trembling I read him a letter that I had written – an honest, unedited version of what had happened and how it had impacted me.

Then, I offered him forgiveness. I explained how I had re-ceived forgiveness through Jesus Christ and that I chose to for-give him for what he had done to me. To say I was shocked at what happened next would be an enormous understatement.

First, he apologized and shared a bit more of his life and what had happened to him at that age – not as an excuse, but an explanation. Then he nearly rendered me speechless by saying that he was a Christian. This was beyond what I could have hoped for! Over those past few years I had prayed for his salvation on numerous occasions, the first being a few months into my counselling. I had been driving home when I suddenly realized that he was destined for hell, and though I hated him for what he did, I wouldn't wish an eternal separation from God on anyone. So I literally *begged* Jesus to save him. I was crying so hard I nearly had to pull the car over as I cried out to God for his salvation. That was two years before this phone call and I had forgotten about it . . . until I asked him when he had become a Christian.

'Two years ago,' he said, pausing – and then he continued: 'It was the strangest thing . . . one day I was driving and I suddenly had this very strong, overwhelming urge to pull into a church and ask the minister about salvation and heaven. And so I did, and he helped me become a Christian that day.'

I cannot prove that the moment I was pleading for his salvation was the moment he pulled into the church car park,[2] but I like to think that while forgiveness was extended from me, salvation was received for him.

Perfect worlds can become shattered, but shattered worlds can be perfected again.

This can only happen in a personal relationship with Jesus Christ and through surrender to the grace and beauty found in the most perfect love we will ever experience. This side of heaven will always have challenges, but a journey out of hiddenness and fear into holiness and love can be created by placing the shattered pieces of our hearts into a beautiful mosaic of redemption and grace – beautifully reflecting a garden from long ago.

Perfection

Living in the modern world, as amazing as it is, challenges our ability to imagine what it was like at the beginning of time. A quick search online will show that the Garden of Eden has been 'found' in Iraq . . . and Tanzania . . . and Antarctica. In other words, nobody knows exactly where it was located. As we will have a new heaven and a new earth in the coming days, personally I don't think we need to be worried about the original location. So, rather than hypothesize about what might be true, let's look at what we know to be true.

The Garden of Eden was created by God for Adam and Eve to dwell in together, having dominion over all the creatures therein and enjoying fellowship with the Father. Like a waiting womb, paradise awaited the seed of promise, created by the love of the Father – its protective walls allowing the children to thrive into purpose. This garden was filled with beauty and perfection. A place where newly created humanity dwelled with their Father: laughter was heard, conversation was had, peace was felt and innocence was birthed.

Yet, perfection and beauty proved too great a temptation to one who had once personified beauty and perfection[3] before his fall. Pride rose in Satan's heart and he was cast out of the presence of God – giving him new boundaries within which to do his work. His new domain became our world, and while he holds no legal right over believers, he continually seeks open doors to barge his way into our lives, thoughts, decisions and relationships – creating division and despair everywhere he goes.

Humanity had recently been created in God's image, with virgin eyes and untainted hearts, but they still possessed free will, and in one unwise moment they chose to trust their future to the one who had thwarted God's will. One question of doubt unsettled all semblance of security, and suddenly all they had known became only what Adam and Eve could remember.

> Suddenly all they had known became only what Adam and Eve could remember.

We have all had times in our lives when what we thought was going to be, turned into something we wished had never been. Perhaps that relationship took a turn for the worse or the employer had different expectations from yours. I believe most people have a moment when the idyllic view of their childhood is shattered by the reality of what constitutes 'normal' in other families. The little girl who never realized that the periodic 'smack' from her father is not biblical, or that the verbal abuse and personal attacks ricocheting among family members is not typical of other families. We only know what we know . . . until we know something different.

Adam and Eve only knew the beauty, wonder, peace and safety of the garden . . . until they didn't. Perfection is not always perfection; in fact, in this world there is no perfection outside the perfect love and grace of God. No person, job, spouse, child, gift or money will ever be perfect enough for beings who were created to be satisfied by perfection himself (God):

For we know in part and we prophesy in part, *but when the perfect comes, the partial will pass away.* When I was a child, I spoke like a child, I thought like a child, I reasoned like a child. When I became a man, I gave up childish ways. For now we see in a mirror dimly, but then face to face. Now I know in part; then I shall know fully, even as I have been fully known. So now faith, hope, and love abide, these three; but the greatest of these is love.[4]

Perfection was never meant to be our aim; otherwise, our aim would become our master because, by its very nature, perfection is not satisfied. It needs more, seeks more and

> Perfection was never meant to be our aim.

always strives to be greater. It compares to those around it and vacillates between the pride of greatness and the shame of weakness. When we put expectations of perfection on ourselves, our spouses, children or friends then we have yoked them (or us) to an expectation that is impossible to reach as a human being living in an earthly world. That is cruelty at best and abuse at worst. Nobody is, or ever will be, perfect – except Jesus Christ.

So, how do we balance the obvious understanding that we will never be perfect with the command given by Jesus in Matthew 5:48: 'Be perfect, therefore, as your heavenly Father is perfect'? If Jesus told us to do it, then certainly perfection is a biblical mandate worthy of pursuit?

Renowned Bible teacher and scholar Paula Gooder gives this explanation:

> So what does this verse mean? The first thing to recognise is that this verse sums up Jesus' teaching on the fulfilling of the law. Matthew 5.17 onwards sets out the new relationship of Jesus' disciples to the law. And it's no easy task. Jesus' expectations of his disciples are of a whole life fulfilling of the law – not just squeaking through by not doing certain things, we are not to think them either. Jesus' new relationship with the law is taxing and far reaching. So verse 48 sums up all teaching on this subject and clearly resonates with the Levitical command to be holy as 'the Lord your God is holy' (Leviticus 19.2). Following is no intellectual exercise; it requires whole-life transformation. We are called to mirror the character of God, not merely to do or say the right things.[5]

Perfection is holiness and holiness comes from the perfected one.

Author Dr Harold W. Perkins says: 'The great advance made by Hebrew thought was in the knowledge of the perfection of God. It is . . . *not [about] the production of a perfect man, but union with the perfection of God*.'[6]

I love that. We cannot be perfect separated from God, but in relationship with a perfect God our own perfection can be worked out.

Did God Really Say?

I remember being a little girl wishing I could marry my father, annoyed that my mother had got there first. Of course, I was so young I didn't fully understand what marriage entailed or that I was a bit young for the commitment. All I knew was that I wanted to be closer to my father, and this thing called marriage seemed the perfect way to do that! The fact I couldn't 'commit' further to him was a tremendous disappointment to my little heart. I wonder if sometimes we feel that way with the Lord?

We want to draw nearer to him, but the reality is that our relationship with him is not going to change in function – we are his children. Yet, as with natural relationships, it can mature in depth. My relationship with my father has deepened over the years, and through the ups and downs of any earthly rela-tionship it has matured far beyond the perception of a child. I have never stopped being his daughter, but thankfully our conversations have moved beyond the self-absorbed world of a little girl. At that time it was only about me, but maturity moves a worldview from selfishness to sonship.[7]

We can be quick to judge God's first children, but we would be wise to remind ourselves that – as with all of us – Adam and

Eve were young and naive. Without delving deep into theological debate, a choice was made and, whatever their reason,
that choice did not reach beyond the realm of curious into the
greater response of obedience.

The first words God spoke over Adam and Eve were to be
fruitful, increase and have dominion.[8] In other words, enlarge
beyond self and leave a legacy of multiplication. The Garden of
Eden was glorious, but it was not finished – there was work to
be done and they were the ones to lead the charge. By growing
in their relationship with the Father they would mature in their
understanding of purpose and be integral to God's plan of ex-
panding his kingdom. What an opportunity!

Sadly, temptation proved too much, and before they knew
it, disobedience had given birth to shame. In Genesis 3:1 we
see the enemy twisting doubt around the truth by asking, 'Did
God really say . . .?', causing temptation to strike its first blow,
followed by verse 6 where we read: 'When the woman saw that
the fruit of the tree was good for food and pleasing to the eye,
and also desirable for gaining wisdom, she took some and ate
it. She also gave some to her husband, who
was with her, and he ate it.'

At that moment, hiding became part of
humanity.

> At that moment,
> hiding became
> part of humanity.

Shame

> *Adam and his wife were both naked, and they
> felt no shame.*

Gen. 2:25

At that moment their eyes were opened, and they
suddenly felt shame at their nakedness. So they
sewed fig leaves together to cover themselves.

Gen. 3:7 NLT

I clearly remember shame and confusion engulfing my little 6-year-old mind after the abuse. It was clear that I hadn't understood what happened, but innately I knew that it was wrong. Equally, Adam and Eve, after succumbing to temptation, could never have fully understood the enormity of their sin, yet between Genesis 2 and 3 we see them begin to experience an emotion they had never felt before: shame.

When God asks where Adam is, the man's shame instantly becomes fear, with blame trotting along behind, because instinctively we like to divert attention off our vulnerability when shame has a foothold in our lives. From the beginning of time, within the first few pages of the Bible, we see shame engulfing the first family, sabotaging their vulnerability and setting up their future for more blame, division and disaster. This shame caused Adam and Eve to cover up and subsequently to hide, because shame prefers darkness to light and works hard to keep us hidden – but we were not created for camouflage.

For Adam and Eve, holiness backed out when hiddenness stepped in, affecting their once carefree and intimate relationship with the Father, creating division and separation, which have been passed on for generations. This is the reason the world is full of people searching for love in the unholiest of places, desperate to fill the gap only their Creator can fill. Shame has caused our vision to be skewed and at times our understanding of the Trinity to be unbalanced.

Throughout this book we will go on a journey – a beautiful journey of discovery – back to the heart of God's original intent: walking in the cool of the day, conversing with his children, laughing about the future.

Seen.

Known.

Loved.

Are you ready?

For Reflection

- 'Perfect worlds can become shattered, but shattered worlds can be perfected again.' Have you experienced this in your own life? If so, how have you seen your world become perfected again?

- How do you envision the Garden of Eden? What would it look like, feel like, smell like to you? (Obviously, nobody knows exactly what it was like, so use your imagination!)

- Can you remember when you first started 'hiding' from God in any way? Why was that?

- Coming out of hiddenness takes bravery. Take some time thinking about why you want to draw nearer to the Lord, and what could be on the other side of your bravery.

2

The Gamble

Then the eyes of both were opened, and they
knew that they were naked. And they sewed fig
leaves together and made themselves loincloths.

Gen. 3:7 ESV

Years ago one of my mentors said to me, 'Jen, we are all on this journey together. Today I may be helping you, but one day you will be helping me.' At the time I thought that I had nothing to offer her as she was so much wiser and more experienced than me. Then a few years later her house incurred extensive damage from a fire and her marriage went through a challenging season. It was then that I realized the truth of her words – we need one another. It isn't about having all the answers or being the wisest of the bunch; sometimes it is simply about showing up, listening to each other and crying together.

Although we don't know each other very well I am going to be vulnerable with you early in the book. Because vulnerability, when based on trust, builds intimacy . . . and I believe I can trust you!

One thing that I dislike about myself is my eyelashes. I was born with bright-red hair, which eventually became strawberry-blonde and now has morphed to a mixture of blonde highlights that seem to change with the seasons. I love my natural hair colour; I don't love my extremely blonde eyelashes. Without mascara you cannot even tell that I own a pair of eyelashes – you only see pupils staring out of a skull, naked and unprotected. A bit like the emoji with the shocked face. For that reason, you will never see me walk out of the house without those lashes wrapped up in a coat (or four) of mascara!

The enemy knows our weak spots and will do everything he can to exploit them, so what may be an innocent comment to one person can become a heart-piercing jibe to another. This became real to me when several years ago someone who had expressed interest in me for a long time, and had kissed me the night before, nonchalantly said: 'So, what do you look like *without* [heavy emphasis on that word] make-up?' It was said with an understated arrogance and a strange curiosity to know what he would potentially have to look at one day, if this thing went any further. I should have walked out right there and left Mr Ego to himself.

But instead my insecurity mumbled out a half-hearted, wimpy 'Oh, of course I'm still beautiful, ha!', laughing unconvincingly, as if I didn't believe a word I was saying . . . which I didn't. His response? He nodded, said nothing, and looked away quite concerned.

I remember thinking, *If I had dark eyelashes then he would still think I was beautiful. It's these stupid blonde, non-existent eyelashes that are keeping me from marriage.* Looking back I can see how he was in the wrong for even asking the question (if a man doesn't want me because of what I look like without make-up, then I don't need that kind of shallowness in my world!), but at the time it created an opportunity for me to feel ashamed, embarrassed and ugly.

The insidious nature of the media, politics, bullying, social media and fake news has created a society which is fast becoming immune to anything real and authentic. Why be authentic when we can look so much better filtered?

> Why be authentic when we can look so much better filtered?

Removing authenticity terminates transparency, creating a world saturated with uncertainty. How can I trust you if I'm not sure it is the real you? If someone becomes attracted to us based on a filter, what will happen when they see beyond the filter to real life?

We *all* have filters that we carry around with us every day – physically, emotionally, spiritually and mentally. None of us see our world through perfected understanding; instead we all see through a glass dimly. We filter truth through our senses, experiences, judgments, biases and beliefs. In fact, it is impossible to live without filters in the world – they guide us and help determine our destiny, for good or bad.

But intentionally living behind filters, refusing to let ourselves be known without them, converts filters into prison bars.

Intimacy

'Are you very intimate with the Lord?' she asked. I nearly choked in embarrassment.

'Intimacy' and 'Lord' in the same sentence? I was mortified at the thought, which was obvious by my now bright-red face. The question was innocent – simply asking for information – yet unbeknown to the questioner, and to me at the time, it was a question which would literally change my life.

The traumatic experience I shared in the last chapter clearly shaped my view of the world in many different ways. One of the most obvious was in the way that I saw intimacy. In my mind, intimacy equalled sex. End of story. I realize it was a very narrow way to see things and perhaps I am unusual in that respect, but I believe many people have a skewed version of intimacy, for different reasons.

Sharing our hearts and souls, let alone our physical body, with another human being takes tremendous vulnerability and trust – at least if we share it unhindered and without walls. This also takes time. Trust cannot be forced; it must be developed. I remember being new to a group of people where the leader said 'You just need to trust us', after I had known them for an extremely short period of time. They hadn't done anything to destroy my trust, but I didn't feel comfortable throwing caution to the wind and trusting with abandonment. I remember thinking it wasn't that I *didn't* trust them, but that I was in the process of *building* trust with them. Those are two different mindsets and I think the second one exercises wisdom, not scepticism.

Expecting someone to trust us because we believe that we are trustworthy is to limit the other person's ability to choose, and choice is vital in love. Real love gives someone space, time and an atmosphere that cultivates a safe environment where risk is free to roam, without fear. Should we err on the side of trusting someone until they are proven untrustworthy? Yes, of course I think we should – within reason. But to expect full trust immediately seems naive to me and, more importantly, it removes the joy of the journey. The early days of love are beautiful because there is such expectation, excitement and opportunity to discover.

> Expecting someone to trust us because we believe that we are trustworthy is to limit the other person's ability to choose, and choice is vital in love.

(At least this is what I've been told as my 'blonde-eyelash-loving hunk of wonderfulness' has yet to appear in my life!)

Early love has each one discovering nuances about the other, and little quirks become cute and endearing (until you're married, and then from what I hear they eventually morph into annoying). Older love, experienced by those who have been married for thirty, forty and fifty or more years, has a depth of trust only time can cultivate. After so many years (often) the annoying habits have now been accepted as part of a unique personality, and somehow without them, the one you love would not be . . . the one you love.

That is the beautiful journey only time, trust and intimacy can develop.

A Bridge of Trust

Unsurprisingly, the Bible has some things to say on this subject. In Psalm 118:8 we read: 'It is better to take refuge in the LORD than to trust in humans.'

King David experienced this first-hand when his son betrayed him, his own king (Saul) tried to kill him, and even his close advisor (Ahitophel) turned on him. Though we don't know for certain if he wrote the psalm, it clearly could be written by him. The psalm describes one who is being attacked and abused, yet whose trust is in the Lord, seeing him as good and worthy of praise. That is the balance we must keep when we have been hurt by another: God is still good, even when the actions of others are not.

Jesus also had something to say about trust: 'Now while he was in Jerusalem at the Passover Festival, many people saw the signs he was performing and believed in his name.

But Jesus would not entrust himself to them, for he knew all people.'[1]

Interestingly, the word 'believed' and 'entrust' are the same Greek word (*pisteúō*) and can mean both 'self-based belief' and 'faith-based belief', with the context explaining which is appropriate. So, in the above verse we see that the people at that time had faith in Jesus and the message he was bringing because of the miracles that he did; but simultaneously, he knew that the heart of humanity is fickle and that there would come a day when the ones who praised became the ones who persecuted. A quote I've seen on numerous social media feeds over the years references Bill Johnson, leader of Bethel Church in Redding, California, as saying: 'If you don't live by the praise of men you won't die by their criticism.'

Another way to say that is we must never let the praise or flattery of other people be the bridge upon which trust is built. Remember the serpent in the garden – he tempted the first humans with the idea of becoming like God and knowing both good and evil. The bridge of flattery became the road to destruction, not only for Adam and Eve, but for all of humanity to follow. If trust can only be developed over time, then intimacy cannot be cultivated overnight, even with the Lord.

> Never let the praise or flattery of other people be the bridge upon which trust is built.

I sense that for some of you shame may be saying you are not spiritually where you 'should' be, according to your, or someone else's, timetable. Perhaps you have veered off left and right over the years and allowed the distractions of the world to pull you from the depth of God's word; or you see someone else your age further along spiritually or doing something on a wider scale, and the comparison creates feelings of unworthiness and failure. Consequently, you may feel left behind spiritually and lacking in maturity. Perhaps it's time to stop hiding and stop allowing shame to have any say over your mind and heart; instead, risk the belief that freedom is possible.

Today, you can begin cultivating your 'personal garden' – taking ownership, changing the landscape and atmosphere, returning to the freedom and beauty found in the original design of our relationship with God. You have not been forgotten, nor has the Lord rejected or given up on you. Quite the opposite really; he is eagerly waiting for the time when you return, remove the mask and receive his grace. Perhaps this is a new beginning on your journey of intimacy – this time based on truth, not pretence.

That very revelation changed my life.

Grace

Adam and Eve were uncovered and unashamed for the first two chapters of the Bible. They were created for dominion and relationship, intended for royal robes of righteousness. As they were gambling with the goodness of God, grace stood at attention, eager to step into purpose – as seen in 2 Timothy 1:9–10:

> He has saved us and called us to a holy life – not because of anything we have done but because of his own purpose and grace. This grace was given us in Christ Jesus before the beginning of time, but it has now been revealed through the appearing of our Saviour, Christ Jesus, who has destroyed death and has brought life and immortality to light through the gospel.

Did you notice that it says from before time began, grace was planned? God always has a plan. We see it in the Old Testament through Noah and the flood, Abraham and Isaac, and many other examples. Grace culminated in the fullness of purpose

through Jesus Christ when he destroyed
death and brought us eternal life through

> God always has a
> plan.

his salvation. This is a grace which sees
people as they were originally designed, not as they have chosen
to become.

And as John Bevere explains below, grace in its fullest form
goes beyond salvation to our empowerment, in order to fulfil
the will of God on this earth:

> God's grace is sufficient to help us overcome any hardship, for grace
> empowers us to go beyond our natural ability. Yet most believers see
> grace as merely a cover-up for sin and a ticket into heaven. No won-
> der more believers aren't distinguishing themselves as radiant lights
> in a dark world – there is nothing to radiate! But when we truly
> grasp that God's grace is His empowering presence in our lives, we
> are able to take up the weapons He has placed before us.[2]

We aren't simply forgiven from sin, but
empowered to holiness. There's a vast dif-

> We aren't simply
> forgiven from sin,
> but empowered
> to holiness.

ference between the two, far more than
semantics. Choosing to see ourselves empowered to become Christ-like, rather than
a 'sinner saved by grace', opens the door for our faith to be
activated and our expectation to arise. We are not fighting from
a place of sin, but we are fighting from a place of victory –
victory gained by Jesus Christ at the cross and freely given to us
at salvation. A victory saturated with the mercy of heaven.

Mercy's Kiss

The gamble Adam and Eve made with the enemy changed
history; the decision we make with grace changes destiny.

Hebrews 4:16 says: 'Let us then approach God's throne of grace with confidence, so that we may receive mercy and find grace to help us in our time of need.' I particularly like The Passion Translation: 'So now we come freely and boldly to where love is enthroned, to receive mercy's kiss and discover the grace we urgently need to strengthen us in our time of weakness.'

Isn't that beautiful? We are approaching mercy's kiss, receiving strength and grace from a throne of love.

Mercy's kiss clothed Adam and Eve.

Mercy's kiss instructed Noah to build a boat.

Mercy's kiss held back Abraham's hand from wielding the knife.

Mercy's kiss guided the stone to the head of Goliath.

Mercy's kiss rained down manna for forty years.

Mercy's kiss positioned Joseph in the palace.

Mercy's kiss strengthened Joshua.

Mercy's kiss restored Job.

Mercy's kiss loved the prostitute.

Mercy's kiss freed the demoniac.

Mercy's kiss embraced Judas Iscariot.

Mercy's kiss lay on the cross.

Mercy's kiss rose from the grave.

Mercy's kiss intercedes for us, even now.

Mercy's kiss is waiting to say: 'Welcome home.'

The gamble released devastation, darkness and demons upon the earth, but the kiss of heaven came to comfort even the most wounded of warriors.

We mustn't allow the gamble in the garden to destroy our understanding of grace on earth: grace wins.

For Reflection

- What kinds of filters do you use in your life? Do they change depending on who you are around?

- What does intimacy mean to you? What does spiritual intimacy look like to you?

- Have you ever been taken in by trusting the bridge of flattery? What was the result?

- How do you see the term 'mercy's kiss' worked out in your own life?

3

The Gap

*I looked for someone among them who would
build up the wall and stand before me in the gap
on behalf of the land so that I would not have to
destroy it, but I found no one.*

Ezek. 22:30

'Mind the gap.'

Living in London, I heard that phrase on numerous occasions. The first few times it was cute and quintessentially English, the next hundred times reminded me of my love for London, and the following 10,453 times it was simply a reminder that I was a great distance under the earth, stuck in a metal tube with hundreds of other people who (except for the odd tourist) didn't want to be there!

Some gaps are necessary; they allow breathing space, help us stay a respectable distance from one another, and create safety on the roads. Have you ever stood next to somebody who didn't understand the natural distance of personal space? I meet many new people on a regular basis and there have been several times I have wanted to scream 'Mind the gap, buddy, mind the gap!' I have nearly sashayed around a room trying to get a bit more space from someone who was oblivious to the lack of gap. Can I get an 'amen'?

Gaps can also be dangerous – falling in-between one can prove harmful at best and deadly at worst. I've read numerous news stories of people who have fallen into the gap on the Underground, strangers pulling them to their rescue just before the train starts to move. Or those who have got stuck in gaps while climbing mountains, unable to free themselves from a narrow space.

We would do well to note (and respect) the gaps in our lives, and relationships.

Adam and Eve's decision created a gap that has spanned generations. This gap was not from the heart of God, but from the choice of human beings – creating a space only love could fill. When Adam and Eve sinned they made a decision to rebel against the one request of the Father: do not eat from the tree of the knowledge of good and evil. In a garden filled with lush beauty, trees, animals, vast colours and beautiful smells, they chose to do the one act forbidden them. The temptation was too strong and the curiosity too deep, because gaps often begin innocently – one decision at a time.

Relational gaps can take formation after one sharp comment or one selfish decision. They appear when comfort with one another becomes entitlement to one another. When we stop saying 'I love you', 'I forgive you' or 'Thank you', and instead fill the conversation with complaints, arguments and frustration, we have started moving away from intimacy and towards autonomy. The gaps may appear small and harmless, but it doesn't take long for them to create valleys of division. If you have ever experienced downhill skiing as an amateur, you will know that as you slowly (or quickly, as is often the case) descend the slope, your feet may decide to 'sightsee' on opposite sides of the hill . . . a small gap becomes increasingly wide (and painful) quite quickly. At least that's what I've heard . . .

While a gap in skiing may be painful, it can be deeply damaging when it comes to relationships. The longer the gaps are ignored, the wider misunderstandings grow. The more misunderstandings grow, the wider the distance becomes. A wide gap presents ample opportunity for the enemy to infiltrate the garden of our relationships, filling the space with lies and deception, planting weeds among the beauty.

> If we don't tend to the gaps, we will be forced to deal with the damage.

If we don't tend to the gaps, we will be forced to deal with the damage.

Moses

> *Since then, no prophet has risen in Israel like Moses, whom the LORD knew face to face . . .*

> *Deut. 34:10*

Because Moses was described in the Bible as one who spoke with God face to face, we will be studying and exploring his life and journey throughout this book; there is much to learn from this humble man about intimacy!

One intriguing note of interest is the fact that hiding was a key theme throughout Moses' life – starting as a baby and continuing as an adult. After three months of being hidden in his parents' home, he was set in a basket and strategically placed in the River Nile. The faith of his parents trusted him to be kept safe, which he was, after being rescued by the daughter of Pharaoh (the ruler of Egypt). His identity was hidden in the background as he grew up a son of royalty, until the day his heritage came out of hiding and he murdered an Egyptian who was beating an Israelite slave.

The letter to the Hebrews says: 'By faith Moses, when he had grown up, refused to be known as the son of Pharaoh's daughter. He chose to be ill-treated along with the people of God rather than to enjoy the fleeting pleasures of sin.'[1]

His true identity as a Hebrew came out of hiding, but as a result of his actions he physically stepped back into hiding again. Leaving his title and riches behind him, Moses headed for Midian, where he lived many years in isolation as a shepherd to his father-in-law's sheep. A burning bush called him out of hiding and he boldly approached the new Pharaoh of Egypt to 'let his people go'. After a miraculous escape through the Red Sea, Moses found himself, yet again, living the life of limbo – leading millions of his people around the desert, in obscurity, for the next forty years. (The following chapters will explore all of this in more detail.)

We all have themes in our lives and there are many reasons for this, which we are not going to explore here, but some themes (or patterns or habits) can be spiritual, others subconscious, some generational and others habitual. I don't believe God 'condemns' us to patterns in our lives (e.g. Moses stayed in the desert and never saw the Promised Land because of his own sin of anger, not because it was God's intention), but we can be susceptible to certain patterns if we are not aware of them and choose to change. For example, we know that it can be common for someone who has grown up in a home with an abusive father to marry someone who is an abusive husband. This is certainly not always the case, but we tend to find common traits in those we marry or have close relationship with, and the environments in which our identity was initially formed.

Thankfully, through counselling, prayer, a deeper understanding of our identity in Christ, changing our thinking and speaking patterns, accountability and other forms of support there is freedom available. But we must recognize these patterns in order to make a change.

Blind Spots

In the last chapter we touched on filters that we carry with us; here I want to mention blind spots – those negative areas of our lives that we are unaware exist (thus the term '*blind* spot'), yet which can be obvious to those closest to us . . . and, at times, even those watching from a distance. There was someone I once knew who had an enormous blind spot relationally. This person could not see what was remarkably obvious to everyone else: their fear of commitment and intimacy. Numerous pastors, leaders and friends tried to hold up a mirror, only to be told the mirror was lying. Well, unless you are at a circus, mirrors don't lie! Sadly this person has continued to live, as far as I'm aware, in a state of denial to this day, leaving a trail of confusion, pain and damage behind them as they (somewhat) ignorantly carry on within the safety of their selfishness.

Are there people in your life who have repeatedly tried talking to you about an area of behaviour or belief that you cannot see? Do you find yourself saying phrases such as 'You just don't understand me', 'It isn't *my* fault', 'You're wrong', instead of taking what has been said before the Lord and asking him to reveal the truth to you? One person's opinion can be incorrect, but if we have several people, whom we trust and who have our best interest at heart, saying the same thing to us, then it is highly likely there is a blind spot at work.

Filters are usually intentional; blind spots are often habitual. We choose to filter a photo, and we can choose to filter what others see about us – living a persona that perhaps is not accurate, but at least brings comfort.

> Filters are usually intentional; blind spots are often habitual.

Just as there are blind spots in driving, which are dangerous and the reason we must be alert and aware at all times, so there are blind spots in our emotions or habits that can be equally dangerous – both to us and to others.

The Bible says in 1 John 1:6–8:

> If we claim to have fellowship with him and yet walk in the darkness, we lie and do not live out the truth. But if we walk in the light, as he is in the light, we have fellowship with one another, and the blood of Jesus, his Son, purifies us from all sin. If we claim to be without sin, we deceive ourselves and the truth is not in us.

We are responsible for asking the Holy Spirit if there are any blind spots in our lives, and then to repent (turn from) acting in a way that is not in line with Scripture. Beth Moore says:

> Christian leaders who can't be regularly challenged will overtime unhinge. Who gets to say to us, 'You're getting bizarre'? If we only listen to those who think just like us, we'll never think we're wrong. If you and I can't think of the last time we were wrong, something is really wrong. We're losing our grip of reality.[2]

This not only applies to Christian leaders, but to all of us. If we cannot remember the last time we were wrong, then I suggest blind spots are at work in our lives! We must not take it to the other extreme, where we are 'navel gazing' and obsessed with saying sorry for things we do not need to apologize for (a British pastime!), but if the Holy Spirit highlights something or we feel the conviction in our spirit, then that is the time to come before the Lord, receiving his beautiful grace and forgiveness.

King David is a good example of someone who had a blind spot. Even though he regularly went before the Lord in honest repentance, he still couldn't see his sin. I like how clearly the Amplified Bible records his writings in Psalm 19:12–14 (AMPC):

> Who can discern his lapses *and* errors? Clear me from hidden [and unconscious] faults. Keep back Your servant also from presumptuous sins; let them not have dominion over me! Then shall I be blameless, and I shall be innocent *and* clear of great transgression. Let the words of my mouth and the meditation of my heart be acceptable in Your sight, O Lord, my [firm, impenetrable] Rock and my Redeemer.

David recognizes that we all have hidden and unconscious faults, presumptuous sins, which can take place without our knowledge. Here was a man who committed both murder and adultery, oblivious to the depth of his sin and depravity, until Nathan the prophet pointed it out to him.[3]

At that point he repented and took responsibility for his actions, shining a light on his sin and walking free.

Without ownership of our actions we cannot close the gap between blindness and freedom – and ownership involves accepting responsibility for the journey.

Without ownership of our actions we cannot close the gap between blindness and freedom.

Hiddenness

There was a season in my life when God called me to a place of hiddenness. I had recently been thrust into an uninvited transition and was seeking God for my next step. One morning I was teaching a small group of ladies, when a lovely, elderly saint whom I'd never met before prophesied that I was being put into the cleft of a rock and hidden for one year. (You know those times when someone gives you a prophetic word that you would rather not have? This was one of those times. Thanks, sweetie, but . . . no thanks.)

I had been struggling financially for several months and the thought of this continuing for a year was a bit more than I could handle. I received it kindly, but put it on the shelf and hoped that she was a false prophet.

A month later I was doing my devotions when I read Exodus 33, which explains that God put Moses in the cleft of the rock. The Spirit of God prompted me to look up the word 'cleft'. I saw that it meant 'division' and I noticed that in division was the very place God's goodness passed over (we will look at this in more detail towards the end of the book). As I had recently experienced division in some personal relationships, this spoke volumes to me and I knew the Lord was confirming to me that he indeed was hiding me . . . but that it would work out for my good.

But a *year*, Lord . . . are you *sure*?

One month later I was visiting a pastor friend of mine whom I don't see often, but for whom I have tremendous respect. As we talked for a few minutes she suddenly interrupted me and said, 'Sorry, Jen, to interrupt you, but I have to say something. I've never given this word before, but the Lord is very clearly saying the word "cleft of a rock" and "hiddenness" to me . . . does that mean anything to you?'

With a sigh I thought to myself, *A year it is then . . .* and I chose to surrender to the journey God was taking me on, knowing that a good God leads us *through* valleys and towards blessings on the other side.

The encouraging part of the word was that the older woman had also said that after the year of hiddenness she saw a rocket taking off and she felt everything would shift after that and go to another level. I clung to that word for a year through *tremendous* difficulty and then, literally a year from that time (almost to the day), everything in my life changed and I've not looked back since.

Hiddenness for a season can be pivotal, but for a lifetime will become paralysing.

> Hiddenness for a season can be pivotal, but for a lifetime will become paralysing.

A pause in music or dialogue can often be inserted for dramatic effect, letting us know that what follows is important and worthy of note. It's the same way in life. Often what feels like a pause is simply a time for us to catch our breath before the Lord shifts us to a new season, or speaks a new word, and he wants to make sure we are still enough to hear what he has to say. The next time you sense a gap in your spiritual journey, realize it may be there to create an opportunity for God to fill it in the most unusual way, bringing about the most spectacular results.

Some gaps must be avoided, others explored. Lean in and listen for the leading of Holy Spirit to discern which it is because, as we see with Moses, God probably has something important to say.

For Reflection

- Have you had a time in your life when there was a 'gap' in a relationship that needed mending? How did you do that?

- If hiding was a theme in the life of Moses, what would you consider to be a theme of your life? Why?

- Has anyone ever told you that you have a blind spot? Would you be willing to ask a close friend or a spouse what blind spots you have, if any?

- What situations or circumstances cause you to 'hide' from God?

Part Two

Hiding

4

I Was Born This Way

*And she became pregnant and gave birth to a
son. When she saw that he was a fine child, she
hid him for three months.*

Exod. 2:2

'You can't see me!' Harry shouted . . . while standing directly
in front of me.

At the mere age of 3, Harry believed that covering his own
eyes meant everyone else was blinded to his presence. He was
too young to realize his was the only sight to be hindered as he
giggled at our sudden, apparent blindness.

Isn't that the way in life sometimes? As we saw in the last
chapter, we casually assume the blindness is only found in
others, never in ourselves. Didn't Jesus allude to that when he
spoke about taking a speck of sawdust out of someone else's eye
when there's still a plank in yours?[1]

So, pretending that I couldn't see Harry, I repeatedly said
out loud, 'Where is Harry?', 'Has anyone seen Harry?', 'I wonder where Harry went?' . . . and all the while my heart was smil-
ing as I looked at the very one I was seeking. I have a sneaky
suspicion God may have felt a bit like that with Adam and Eve

when he was in the garden 'seeking' them. He saw his children playing a game of hiddenness in which they would always be found, because the one who loved them more than life itself would never let them out of his sight. They couldn't know it at the time, but in their disobedience they were still in the safest place they could be – his affection and his love. When he asked them 'Where are you?', he wasn't searching for information; he was longing for relationship: The Father knew exactly where his children were located – and why.

I feigned surprise when Harry suddenly said 'Here I am!' And with glee I took him into my arms and gave him the biggest hug I could, enjoying his giggles of triumph at my inability to discover what he thought had been hidden.

Because that's what love does: it covers; it embraces; it forgives.

It feigns surprise when it has seen the obvious all along, knowing that at one time or another, we will all need to be found.

> Because that's what love does: it covers; it embraces; it forgives.

Identity Void

We live in a self-obsessed and identity-deprived generation.

According to a *Telegraph* article, the number of selfies taken a day equates to 1 million – 1 million pictures of ourselves *every day*.[2] I'll say it again: we live in a self-obsessed and identity-deprived generation!

Recently on the news was the story of a 69-year-old Dutch man who has decided he legally wants to be 49 years old. Not much surprises me any more, but I was gobsmacked when I read that story. How on *earth* does someone think they can simply change their age and be born in a different year, let alone generation? It would be humorous if it was not so ludicrous. Clearly one cannot simply change one's age. Just because you *think* you are a certain age does not automatically mean you *are* that age, because it is impossible to replace what has been divinely designed . . . and therein lies the issue. Our society (in the West at least) has become so used to having everything we want that when we are told we cannot have it, we either disregard the rules or we create a way around them. It is selfishness at its core, leading us further and further away from the integrity of the truth. A world separated from truth will always create its own version of reality. Simply wishing or deciding I am an Olympic runner does not make me one, because that is not who I've been designed to be.

> A world separated from truth will always create its own version of reality.

The Dutch man said that he feels and looks like the age of 49, therefore he wants to be legally recognized as that. Rather than being grateful for the blessing of ageing well, he is stepping into denial and avoiding truth. He says it is because of a dating site he wants to engage in, to date women who are twenty years younger than him (because that's a great way to start a relationship – by *lying* about your age!).

That is a good example of what wrongly filling a gap looks like – meditating on a false reality long enough that it becomes our version of a true reality.

In his book *Victory Over the Darkness* Neil Anderson says:

Understanding your identity in Christ is essential for living the Christian life. People cannot consistently behave in ways that are inconsistent with the way they perceive themselves. You don't change yourself by your perception. You change your perception of yourself by believing the truth. If you perceive yourself wrongly, you will live wrongly because what you are believing is not true . . . Next to a knowledge of God, a knowledge of who you are is by far the most important truth you can possess.[3]

Without a true knowledge of who we are in Christ, we may try to fill that identity gap with a filtered view of how we want to be perceived, because we are afraid the truth may not be good enough. If I believe that I have been wronged in my age, sexuality, job, marriage, friendship and so on, then I will seek an identity that validates my belief system. When our identity is found in Jesus Christ then we will act from a place of security; the same security that Adam and Eve originally had in the garden, as they walked in the cool of the day with the Lord. A security that says we are accepted as we are, protected and cherished, loved and wanted. A security that will never leave us feeling abandoned or orphaned. A security that draws us out of threatening waters and places us into a promise of provision, setting us up for a future of fulfilment and purpose.

Surrender

Let's return to Moses, chosen by the Lord as the deliverer of his people, but first needing deliverance in his own life. In the days of Moses' birth, Pharaoh noticed that the Israelites were multiplying quickly, so out of fear he decreed to the midwives that any Hebrew boys must be murdered immediately after birth. The midwives, however, feared God more than a man so they refused to obey, saying that the Hebrew women gave birth so quickly there wasn't time for the midwives to arrive and terminate the child. Not to be deterred, Pharaoh commanded that all sons born to Hebrew women should be cast into the River Nile and drowned. Soon after this decree, a Levite woman gave birth to Moses and after noticing that he was 'beautiful', chose to hide him for three months. After three months had passed, she and her family realized hiding was no longer an option, so they chose surrender and trust. We read the story in Exodus 2:4–10:

> His sister stood at a distance to see what would happen to him. Then Pharaoh's daughter went down to the Nile to bathe, and her attendants were walking along the river-bank. She saw the basket among the reeds and sent her female slave to get it. She opened it and saw the baby. He was crying, and she felt sorry for him. 'This is one of the Hebrew babies,' she said. Then his sister asked Pharaoh's daughter, 'Shall I go and get one of the Hebrew women to nurse the baby for you?' 'Yes, go,' she answered. So the girl went and got the baby's mother. Pharaoh's daughter said to her, 'Take this baby and nurse him for me, and I will pay you.' So the woman took the baby and nursed him. When the child grew older, she took him to Pharaoh's daughter and he became her son. She named him Moses, saying, 'I drew him out of the water.'

If you are tired of hiding, it may be time for surrender.

> If you are tired of hiding, it may be time for surrender.

Some of us have hidden for years – hidden from friends, opportunity, risk, our spouse and even ourselves. There are many reasons we hide, or stay hidden, but all have a link to the fear of rejection and/or pain. If we are known – seen – we become vulnerable; and past experience shows us that vulnerability involves pain.

Therefore, choosing to hide and not be seen takes precedence over being known, to our own emotional detriment. As I said earlier, I believe there are seasons when a type of hiding may be necessary for healing – but it is never meant to become a lifestyle.

Growing Up

As with Jesus, we don't know a tremendous amount about Moses' growing-up years. There is a period of silence between the time he is weaned by his mother and the time he chooses to kill the Egyptian. Yet knowing that he grew up in a royal household leads us to make some educated assumptions, which are explained in more detail here:

> Adopted by a royal princess and raised in the palace of the Pharaoh, Moses received the best education the ancient world could offer at that time. The royal princes and princesses, their cousins, the children of favored royal officials, as well as some of the children of vassal kings, were entrusted to the royal tutor. The children of the royal school would have learned not only to read and to write but would also have been taught to write hieratic, the 'shorthand' version of the hieroglyphic script as well as the Babylonian cuneiform script, the diplomatic language of the ancient Near East. In addition, they studied mathematics, astronomy, and the origins of the gods, with unlimited access to the wealth of texts in the royal archives. Children of the royal family like Moses, not in the direct line of succession, were usually trained for service in the diplomatic corps or as military leaders (Fletcher, *Chronicle of a Pharaoh,* pages 24–27). Moses' education in Egypt would have more than prepared him for his role as redeemer/political leader/military general to the embryonic nation of Israel.[4]

Though Moses was separated from his birth parents, he was adopted into security, wealth and prestige as the grandson of the most powerful man on earth at that time (Pharaoh). Ironically, Moses was raised in the home of his people's arch-enemy. I read recently that it would be like the deliverer of the Jews being raised as Adolf Hitler's grandson.[5] As an Israelite, it is remarkable that Moses survived, knowing the hatred for the people of Israel at that time; but when God has his hand on a life, he will bring about purpose regardless of the enemy's schemes.

I remember my mother telling me not to be concerned if I was not in the 'popular' group at school (easy for an adult to say), because those who were popular in school often find the real world challenging. The 'fish bowl' gets bigger, and suddenly the world doesn't revolve around them any more, which can be a shock to someone who hasn't yet had to handle rejection. Alternatively, those who were overlooked or teased as a child are often the ones who excel because they learn what it is to face adversity and overcome challenge at an early age. It wasn't particularly comforting to me as a 15-year-old, but as an adult I saw what she meant – and she was right.

Moses was the grandson of the most powerful man in Egypt, and had tremendous privilege as a result of others' generosity. However, there came a time when privilege was not enough, when those same Egyptians whom Moses had grown up with, lived among, and played with as a child wanted to kill him – thus uncovering what he had been trying to hide all these years, his story.

Your Story

We all have a story.

It is what makes us unique, defines our personality and helps us empathize with others who may have walked a similar journey. A story does not need to be extraordinary to be impactful; it simply needs to be lived, embraced and owned. The more we own our story, not allowing fear or shame to call the shots in our life, the freer we are to pursue and experience all that God has destined us to fulfil.

You may have had some challenging circumstances early in life. Perhaps you were adopted; experienced abuse as a child; lived through trauma, death or rejection. It may have been a physical issue that limited your ability to be accepted as 'normal', or possibly your family moved so often that staying isolated was easier than making friends you would soon need to leave. Anything that makes us different as a child sets us up for ridicule, and – as we know – children can be the worst critics of all. Now more than ever, bullying has become a stain on our society.

A report from the YMCA in February 2018 gives the following statistics:

> More than half (55%) of young people have been bullied about the way they look, with two fifths of those experiencing this bullying at least once a week.

> Most of the bullying focusses on weight and body shape, with 60% of young people admitting they tried to change their appearance after being bullied and 24% said they reduced the amount they ate or went on a diet. In some cases the effect was more severe with one in ten of those being bullied about their looks having suicidal thoughts and 9% saying they self-harmed as a result.[6]

Challenges, difficulties, tragedy, pain, rejection and hurt weave themselves into each and every one of our stories. Comparing trauma is futile and blame will never birth blessing. Our story is our story, and what we do with our story is what shapes our legacy.

In my other books I have alluded to some of the challenges I had growing up: I was intensely shy, always filled with deep fear and insecurity, consumed with self-hatred; I battled anorexia and bulimia, and tried to commit suicide on more than one occasion. Do I wish I had been different? Yes. Do I wish I had had a healthier self-confidence and awareness as a young adult? Absolutely. Do I wish I had never been sexually abused as a child and teenager? Of course, yes.

But I cannot change those experiences, and living in a state of blame or victimhood will never create a life of freedom, abundance and joy – the life promised us in John 10:10. I have seen many people waste many years of their lives, and sometimes their entire lives, living in a bubble of victimhood, comforted by their grief or pain, allowing one part of their story to become their entire story.

Moses started his life hiding from the enemy – not by his choice, but hiding nonetheless. We cannot run from that which has shaped us, but what has shaped us need not define us.

> We cannot run from that which has shaped us, but what has shaped us need not define us.

For Reflection

- 'We live in a self-obsessed and identity-deprived generation.' Do you agree with this statement? Why or why not?

- What would it look like for you to *fully* surrender to the Lord? In other words, is there any area that is a no-go zone for God in your life?

- How do you think Moses might have felt when he realized he was adopted into royalty and should have been murdered as a baby by the very people he now called family?

- What makes your story unique?

5

The Disconnect

*When Pharaoh heard of this, he tried to kill
Moses, but Moses fled from Pharaoh and went to
live in Midian, where he sat down by a well.*
                                            Exod. 2:15

I was walking to my internship during the morning rush hour
of downtown Chicago traffic when it happened. The normal
buzzing, beeping and busy traffic had come to a complete
standstill – a rarity in the Windy City of America – because
a lame pigeon (meaning injured, not inept) was hobbling his
way towards safety. I knew he would never reach his destination without further injury (i.e. death), so I did what any good
Spirit-filled citizen of God would do: I stepped into the road,
firmly planted my feet and horizontally held out my arms.
I could have been mistaken for a priest giving the benediction
if I hadn't been dressed in jeans and a sweatshirt.

   I made sure both sides of traffic knew they were not allowed
to move until our special guest had arrived safely at the other
side. At first there was confusion, but soon it became annoyance, creating an orchestra of horns telling me off, as only city
people can do. They were busy, had jobs to get to, it was rush

hour traffic and this was . . . a pigeon. I didn't care. It was one of God's creatures and I would not stand by and watch him get flattened, simply because he had a limp.

While I'm not comparing the Israelites to pigeons, they had a limp. They were at an impasse and unable to escape without injury. So when Moses saw that one was being unfairly beaten (as if any beating is ever justified) he took action. Ironically, the same streak of justice flowed through Moses' veins that had been in his mother and father. Hebrews 11:23 says that his parents did not fear the king, which is why they saved their son's life. They were willing to stand up to injustice, as we see Moses doing forty years later for one of his fellow Israelites.

The next two verses of Hebrews 11 go on to say: 'By faith Moses, when he had grown up, refused to be known as the son of Pharaoh's daughter. He chose to be ill-treated along with the people of God rather than to enjoy the fleeting pleasures of sin.'

He chose.

We do not know why Moses intervened on this occasion or why he chose to go as far as murder, but we do know that this choice unravelled a stream of events that would change the course of his life, and even of history itself. By not seeking God and instead making an impetuous and prideful choice, Moses saved one man, yet quite possibly deferred deliverance of a nation by forty more years.

> Position or gifting never justifies an independent spirit.

Position or gifting never justifies an independent spirit.

Without God's direction we can easily be misled, rejoicing in our own works, oblivious to what we could have accomplished if surrendered to God's ways. This was not youthful impetuosity or even unrestrained rage – it was a deliberate choice made by a 40-year-old man who was attempting to solve things on his terms. Of course, he would not have seen it that way (several thousand years of hindsight is a beautiful thing). Moses was acting in line with his calling, but not in line with his character.

Character Counts

Both calling and character must be developed if we want to see the fulfilment of God's plans; a great calling, with lack of character, will restrict kingdom impact. We see this all the time in world leaders, business entrepreneurs, music artists, and so on. Their gifting may be extraordinary, clearly God-given, yet the lack of character means that the impact will be limited to this world and rarely to the next. It reminds me of Matthew 16:26,

> Both calling and character must be developed if we want to see the fulfilment of God's plans.

where Jesus says: 'What good will it be for someone to gain the whole world, yet forfeit their soul? Or what can anyone give in exchange for their soul?'

We often try to rush God's timing to fit our timetable. I once heard someone say, 'Don't trade God's timing for your deadline!' There are always things God knows in his wisdom that we will never understand in our humanity, and trying to force the hand of God is futile; instead, prepare your character to carry your calling, because when God moves, he moves!

So, let me ask you: are you the same person behind closed doors as you are on a Sunday morning? Do your kids see a different response in private from the one they hear in public? Would your social media followers describe you as one who 'acts justly, loves mercy and walks humbly with her God'?[1]

Recently, I have been shocked at what I have seen written on social media – and this from leaders I respect! Words of accusation, negativity, blame, criticism, division, judgment and condemnation. None of which are godly or would help draw others nearer to the truth of the gospel. Yes, we absolutely need to call out injustice and stand up for what is wrong, but the manner in which we do this must not emulate the world. Please, for the sake of the kingdom, refrain from fighting evil with evil, but choose to overcome evil with good.[2]

In that moment when he killed the Egyptian, Moses accomplished what he set out to do – eradicate the enemy and serve justice for his people. But it cost him greatly and propelled him into a life on the outside, hidden and disconnected – a fugitive.

The Fugitive

Recently, my dad and I were talking about the wildfires in California and how difficult it would be to leave your home at short notice, having to pack up everything you needed within a few minutes. My dad said, 'I would take Amber [the dog] and your mother. Everything else pales in comparison.'

Overlooking the fact that he chose to leave the cat behind, he quickly corrected himself: 'And not in that order!' That's good, Dad – I'm glad that Mom takes precedence over the dog.

Fleeing makes us focus.

Moses had to decide what was most important to him, and in that moment it was his life and his future, not his money or his possessions. Quite possibly the princess, his Egyptian mother, had died and so he was more vulnerable to danger than when he was a child. Whatever the reason, Moses knew that freedom was going to be found in leaving all that he had ever known. Have you ever had to make that choice? Those escaping physical or spiritual persecution know what it means to flee, but I also think those choosing to walk out of abusive relationships, unhealthy friendships and controlling environments have tasted the sacrifice of choice. It is easy to criticize the choice of the vulnerable from the armchair of security.

> It is easy to criticize the choice of the vulnerable from the armchair of security.

When staying where we are is more damaging than risking what might be, it could be time to make a move. Please understand I am not endorsing divorce or casually suggesting you remove yourself from a commitment, but I am saying that ignoring the damage will never heal the wound. This includes our relationship with the Lord, which is where real trust ultimately is developed. Because as we trust him, we can more freely trust others without expecting them to give what ultimately only God can give: unconditional love.

Moses had traded a lifetime of royalty for the life of a refugee. He was on the run, couldn't return home, living in the unknown and a stranger wherever he went: it was in that place of uncertainty that he chose to settle, finding home in the most unusual of places. Though I am not comparing my experience to a refugee, I empathize with the challenge of feeling comfortable in a place not necessarily of your choosing.

In the past fifteen years of living in England I have experienced life in Devon, south London, West Yorkshire, north London and Somerset. They, whoever they are, are correct – the north and south of the country are close in distance (relatively speaking) yet worlds apart. For years I have sought to settle, yet the 'cloud would move' and I knew the Lord was asking me to take another step of faith with him. So, up and off we would go to a new city, not knowing what was ahead, but trusting who was in charge.

Last year I moved to Bath, England. London has always had a very special place in my heart and, to be completely honest, I couldn't imagine settling anywhere else. Moving to Bath was not on my agenda or in my plans, so when I knew that it was the Lord's leading I reluctantly, yet obediently, packed up my belongings and stopped asking myself how I felt about it. I had only been in Bath a short time when I was chatting with the Lord about the move and my lack of enthusiasm for leaving the city I loved and moving to yet *another* temporary space (I was living in interim accommodation) – would I *ever* find a place of permanence? The Lord suddenly said: 'Jen, it will be like having two children. You love them both. You love them differently – but you love them both.' He was right. I loved London and I am falling in love with Bath.

I am currently in America writing a portion of this book and, to be completely honest, as much as I love being with my family, I also miss England when I'm here. It's a strange thing to always be home, yet never be home. When I am in America I'm home . . . yet I'm not. And when I am in England I'm suddenly home . . . and yet I'm not.

Through all of this, I have learned that our truest home on earth has to ultimately be where the Lord resides, within our heart, because anywhere else is temporary at best. We have been created for another home, and until we see him face to face in that eternal place, *none* of us are truly home.

Starting Over

Once Moses' cover-up was exposed and he knew that his life was in danger he fled. However justified, murder is murder, and Moses knew that Pharaoh would not look favourably on his actions, regardless of his status, or history, in the royal household.

Therefore, Moses left Egypt and the familiar for Midian and the unknown. It was here that the justice streak that would define his life rose again and he defended seven women at a well:

> Now a priest of Midian had seven daughters, and they came to draw water and fill the troughs to water their father's flock. Some shepherds came along and drove them away, but Moses got up and came to their rescue and watered their flock.
>
> When the girls returned to Reuel their father, he asked them, 'Why have you returned so early today?'
>
> They answered, 'An Egyptian rescued us from the shepherds. He even drew water for us and watered the flock.'
>
> 'And where is he?' Reuel asked his daughters. 'Why did you leave him? Invite him to have something to eat.'
>
> Moses agreed to stay with the man, who gave his daughter Zipporah to Moses in marriage. Zipporah gave birth to a son, and Moses named him Gershom, saying, 'I have become a foreigner in a foreign land.'[3]

After Moses' help, the women arrived home earlier than normal. Their father, Reuel, questioned their expediency, so they explained there was an Egyptian who had come to their rescue. Moses had lived so many years in the royal household that he had been mistaken for the royalty they raised him to become. But he was no longer royalty and, as he saw the women being mistreated, he related to the feeling of being on the outside, overlooked simply because of position.

He had escaped slavery through providence, but his error was taking on the providential role himself and defending others in a manner not endorsed by God. He would not make that mistake this time.

The father, aghast at the thought of this knight in shining armour (or should we say: strong man in Egyptian clothing) sleeping under the stars, ordered his daughters to retrieve the rescuer and bring him home. A father with seven daughters knows a good prospect when he sees one! Moses agreed to stay and soon married and had a child, whom he named Gershom, which means 'sojourner in a foreign land'. Clearly Moses was still missing the familiarity of Egypt and his people.

We all carry themes to our lives and the older we become, if we are observant, the more we will see them play out in a cyclical pattern, leading us onwards and upwards through the various stages of purpose in our lives. This is why it's important to observe experiences, desires, opportunities and gifting – they all form part of the whole. Because purpose is not a destination you arrive at; it is a journey you live out.

As we mature, we should find ourselves responding to similar or familiar circumstances with different choices and greater wisdom. If an experience feels 'familiar' to you, quite possibly it is similar to an experience you went through ten or twenty years prior to this, but God is allowing you to respond differently this time – out of what you have learned over the years. Therefore, never let fear have the last word or convince you that this outcome will be the same as your last trial. That's one of the enemy's most uncreative, yet most popular, lies. Invite God into the present story, listen for his leading and stay obedient to the Spirit.

> Invite God into the present story, listen for his leading and stay obedient to the Spirit.

Moses left royalty for the desert; but, after being called by God, he returned to lead those in the desert towards a royal inheritance – yet they would not leave their slavery behind. This is such an important topic that we will revisit it later in the book: *we must release a slavery mentality if we want to obtain a different outcome for a similar experience.*

In the next few chapters we are going to explore what it looks like to live with a fugitive state of mind, resting between slavery and freedom, because it is imperative that we break a slavery mentality if we want to deepen our spiritual intimacy.

Moses' life finally looked normal to the casual observer, but as much as he might have longed for normality, he was purposed for authority. The Israelites had a limp and were in danger, and Moses had been chosen to bring them safely to the other side.

It is here that Moses' journey truly begins.

For Reflection

- In your life, where do you have a limp? Or what limp have you overcome in your life?

- What character issues is the Lord dealing with at this time in your life? (We *all* have character traits that can be refined!)

- If you had to quickly leave your house in an emergency, what would be the first items you would grab? Why? In other words, what means 'home' to you?

- Have you ever tried to 'help God' by interfering and then getting it terribly wrong?

6

Love Hurts

Can a mother forget the baby at her breast and
have no compassion on the child she has borne?
Though she may forget, I will not forget you!
                                    Isa. 49:15

There are none as vulnerable as a newborn. Beautiful innocence coupled with profound fragility is a reminder of the first
children ever created. As we have seen, their start in life began
in a pure, holy garden filled with peace, joy, companionship
and love. There was no suffering, pain, rejection or negativity;
it was the purest atmosphere of love and acceptance anyone
could ever experience and vastly different from the cultures in
which we live today. Each child shaped by the hand of God,
created for his pleasure and wrapped in his love. A more perfect
start to life has never been, and will never be, found.

We often (for good reason) recoil when we hear stories of
trauma or abuse perpetrated against children, and the younger
the child, the more horrendous the crime. Yet, it's interesting
to note that at the beginning of time it wasn't the child being
rejected, but the parent. The choice made by Adam and Eve
created a distance only death could cross (no pun intended) and

we will never fully know the pain God felt when temptation was offered and sin was birthed.

We do know this: love was the foundation of every decision God made after the rebellion of those first humans. Never once did he respond out of spite or from a sense of rejection or hurt – he loved, because he is love, even in the midst of painful and deliberate rejection. It was the birth of rejection on a scale that we can never fully understand. Not only had God been rejected, but Adam and Eve's choice created a separation that impacted all future generations: the relationship with his children moved from an understood, to an undecided.

> Relationship with his children moved from an understood, to an undecided.

Rejection

If women are fickle in general, teenage girls are 'fickle on steroids'.

Last year when visiting my parents' home, I stumbled upon my diary as a pre-teen and early teenager. It was hilarious to read as I traversed the daily ups and downs of a pre-pubescent girl's emotions. One day was the happiest day of my life, and the next entry had me despairing to the point of not wanting to live. I had new-found sympathy for my parents, or any parent of a teenage girl for that matter!

As I was perusing the plethora of emotions, I noticed that one account was about a young man, older than me, whom I wanted to marry. I thought he was the most handsome boy I had ever seen, and in order to win his affection I would get up at 4.30 a.m. to take a shower, do my hair and apply a bit of make-up before getting in a truck with my father to collect him and go fishing on Lake Michigan. (Having your lipstick on point when you are miles away from civilization is quite important, you know.) Looking back now, it is clear this good-looking young man would have absolutely no interest in an insecure, pre-teen girl like me, but I was prepared, nonetheless.

It's a shock to you I'm sure, but that 'relationship' fizzled out before it even began and soon I was massaging a broken heart and a bruised ego. Then a bit later there was the older boy in school named Eric – tall, dark and handsome. It didn't matter that nearly every girl in school was in love with him, that he was on the football team, and that I was too shy to look at him, let alone speak to him, without hyperventilating. I remember Lionel Richie's song 'Hello' came out about that time, and I would sit and dream for hours of saying hello to Eric in the hallway. Even with Lionel cheering me on (repeat), it never happened. The fear of rejection was simply too great, and 'Goodbye' was a more appropriate rendition of that fleeting never-to-be romance.

It is impossible to come out of hiding and to love without risking rejection. Just ask Jesus.

> It is impossible to come out of hiding and to love without risking rejection. Just ask Jesus.

If anyone knows the pain of loving, it is our Saviour. He loved us enough to leave perfection and settle in suffering – accepting our suffering to give us perfection. He was rejected by his enemies, his friends and even his own family. In his weakest moment, when he most needed the strength of another, he was left to suffer with only a faithful few alongside him – John, his mother, Mary Magdalene, and a few others who believed he was who he said he was. Even the Father appeared to have rejected him in his time of greatest need.

Rejection hurts, but in the long run isolation can hurt even more. Jesus cried out to forgive those who had betrayed him, giving us the most poignant example of how to forgive those who have hurt us.

If we want to come out of hiding and if we want to walk in holiness, we must become intimate with forgiveness. Keeping our emotions locked behind a secure wall of safety and refusing to release those who have caused deep pain in our lives will never create a full and overflowing life. We are created for relationship, and without it – regardless of how we appear outwardly – an inward poverty will take root.

The Paradox

There are times when I am scrolling the BBC news app and I see articles of the 'rich and famous' living in debauchery, spending literally millions of pounds on that which will pass away in this lifetime. Knowing that even a fraction of what was spent on that awards ceremony would help alleviate the suffering of multiplied thousands really troubles me, but it means I have to deliberately stop judging and look instead at my own heart. Mother Teresa said: 'If you judge people, you have no time to love them.'[1] So I examine my own life and ask myself: how much am I giving to those who are facing poverty and disease? Am I intentional in my overflow being spread to nations around the world, providing relief to children suffering unimaginable trauma and hunger?

It is easier to stay in denial because the moment we open our hearts to love, we risk pain. Another well-known Mother Teresa quote says: 'I have found the paradox, that if you love until it hurts, there can be no more hurt, only more love.'[2]

If I'm honest, I'm not there yet. I have experienced wonderful love from my parents, I have known the deep love of friends, and I have tasted and seen that the Lord is good; his love surpasses all other loves and is the one I am most familiar with, and the one this book is written about. But have I loved until it hurts? If I'm honest: sporadically. I'm certain if I were married and had children my answer would be different, but at the moment that's my honest answer. Perhaps some of you can identify with me when I say that I am more comfortable risking love with the Father I know will never leave me or forsake me, than with human beings who cannot honestly give that promise. We have all experienced the departure of another – whether through death, divorce, separation, anger, misunderstanding or simply by choice. It is deeply painful and becomes highly personal.

Yet for others, it may be very different – you are more secure in the love of those you can see than the love of a Father you cannot see. Finally, for some people both may prove too risky, and you prefer to keep the truest part of yourselves hidden behind a wall that neither God nor human is allowed to scale. Joyce Meyer in her book *The Root of Rejection* says:

> God wants to build His walls of protection around us, but as long as we are . . . trying to protect ourselves – God doesn't do it. As God's children, we don't have to labor to protect ourselves. We should place our faith in His protection . . . We can spend so much time trying to protect ourselves from the pain of rejection that we never build a healthy, loving, balanced relationship. But if we allow the Holy Spirit to tear down the wrong walls, then He can activate the protection of God that became available to us through salvation.[3]

How do you risk loving again after you have been hurt? I am certainly no expert, but I know this much: it is a choice. We have been created for relationship and the only way relationships can grow is to risk rejection, because true love never controls, forces or manipulates – it always offers a choice.

The safest place to start is with one who has promised never to leave you and never to forsake you. Remember: God *is* love.

Remember: God is love.

One of my favourite scriptures in the Amplified Bible is found in Isaiah 26:3 (AMPC):

> You will guard him and keep him in perfect and constant peace whose mind [both its inclination and its character] is stayed on You, because he commits himself to You, leans on You, and hopes confidently in You.

As we take steps towards trusting God, both in how we see him and how we think about him, we will find that our hearts become more and more pliable to peace and less filled with anxiety, frustration and negativity. The choice is ours to commit, lean on and hope in what the Bible says is true over what may feel untrue at that moment. God is not like people – he literally cannot lie, so when he says that he will accept and love you unconditionally, that is what he will do. But accepting and loving unconditionally does not mean leaving us as we are.

A Father's love sees who we have been created to be and works to bring us there, risking his own rejection for our future freedom.

Destiny in the Desert

Over the years I have had numerous people question me about my singleness. Being 49 years old and never married I have lost track of the number of times I've been asked, 'Why are you still single?', normally with a sympathetic and sorrowful look on the questioner's face. I've been mocked by a pastor who quipped I must be gay (yes, he actually said that) and even had a female leader in ministry say to me – and I quote – 'I'm sorry this has been your lot in life.'

Really?

My lot in life.

I am not dying; I am not a refugee; I have not lost my home tragically in a fire; I am not lonely . . . I am single. That is not a 'lot in life'; at its core it is a label to help others understand my position relationally. Oh, there is so much I would like to say on that, but I will refrain!

For years I have longed for a husband, a partner, someone to do life alongside and with, in ministry. I have dreamed of us travelling together, taking our family on the road, praying with people and giving our lives to serve the Lord. Being single has not been my choice, nor has it come from a place of selfishness or isolation. Yes, I experienced sexual abuse when I was a child and I had some pretty horrible experiences as a young adult. As a teenager I felt ugly, used, abused and dirty. I wondered what I had done to deserve it and why men treated me this way – seeing me as an object, not a person. I know that some of you can identify with this to an even greater degree, and I am sorry for that. I am sorry that you were used, abused and not respected or loved as you should have been. I am sorry that trust was broken and fear was planted at an age when safety with a parent or adult should have been presumed. I am sorry that innocence was shattered and adulthood accelerated. It should not have happened; it was not the heart of God; it does not define you.

I say this because I have also found that the desert is where we often meet our destiny. In the dark seasons of the soul, when we look shame in the face and confront our greatest fears, we will find freedom waiting, watching and hoping to become part of our journey. Freedom never enters uninvited and will never push its way into our story – it must be written in. So after Moses was rejected

> I have also found that the desert is where we often meet our destiny.

by his people, it was only natural that the desert became his next stop.

It is true – if we love, we will hurt. But if we hide, we will lose.

Have you put up any self-protective walls to keep rejection out and safety in? Are those walls for people, God, or both?

To journey into holiness we must make a deliberate decision to leave hiddenness. As with any step of faith, it may feel uncomfortable and unfamiliar, but I promise your future self will thank you for taking the risk.

And not only your future self, but those on the other side of your fear who will receive their own healing because of what you have chosen to face.

For Reflection

- How do you think God felt when his relationship changed 'from an understood to an undecided'? Have you personally ever experienced that?

- Is it easier for you to trust God's love or the love of a person? Why is that?

- When have you risked loving again after being hurt? What did you learn from that?

- Are you willing to make a deliberate decision to leave hiddenness?

7

How Do I Get Out?

*Out of my distress I called on the LORD; the
LORD answered me and set me free.*

Ps. 118:5 ESV

I clearly remember the day I left prison – the feeling of freedom
was overwhelming.

Before you judge, I personally hadn't been locked up. A col-
league and I were leaving a maximum state facility in America
after having visited a young man who was sent there for attempted
murder. Originally we had met him in a youth detention facility,
until he was released and then made one of the greatest mistakes
of his life after getting high on drugs. It was a rude awakening for
a young man, and to this day I still think of him. Knowing that
we could leave the prison and step into the sunshine and fresh air,
but this teenager had fourteen more *years* left inside, was a feeling
that is difficult to describe. Each time we left I couldn't help but
think: we were not created for prison.

Many people live in a self-imposed prison of fear, locking
themselves behind doors of insecurity. As we know, some even
hide from God – shielding themselves from the very one who
can set them free. I think people often fear that if they let God

in, he is going to bring further pain or try teaching them a lesson. This type of thinking shows a lack of revelation about his love, because the reality is that his love will free us from any prison we have created – whether physical, spiritual, mental or emotional.

> Many people live in a self-imposed prison of fear, locking themselves behind doors of insecurity.

Love is always the answer, but love needs a receiver. We cannot love alone.

Quicksand

I have never seen or experienced quicksand, but I can remember as a teenager being afraid of it. Living in the northern part of the United States near Lake Michigan, I heard stories of those who had become stuck and were unable to escape. With my overactive imagination, I easily convinced myself that if I wasn't careful running through the woods behind our house, the headlines would soon read: 'Local girl leaves home for a walk and is never heard from again. Parents distraught. No clues can be found. She simply . . . vanished.'

As I said, I have an overactive imagination.

I recently watched an online video of a reporter who intentionally got stuck in quicksand on the shores of England (with the coastguard standing next to him on solid ground). It was surprising how quickly he began to sink, and soon it became clear that freeing himself would be impossible; any attempt to do so would only exacerbate the situation as he was literally cemented into a slow-motion suffocation.

Isolating ourselves and thinking *I can handle this on my own* can be a set-up for the quicksand of doubt, despair, depression and hopelessness to get a grip impossible to break. There are situations in life when we cannot – and should not – attempt to break free by ourselves. At those times we need what I like to call 'faith friends'. Those friends whom you can call at any time to stand with you in the pit, and yet who also challenge you to stand in faith for your breakthrough. I think David explains 'pit life' well in Psalm 40:2 where he says: 'He lifted me out of the slimy pit, out of the mud and mire; he set my feet on a rock and gave me a firm place to stand.' Sometimes the only way out of impossibility is to introduce it to the God of possibility.

The Israelites had been stuck in the quicksand of slavery, as it were, for several hundred years, with no hope of escaping. In fact, the harder they worked, the more severe their punishment. It was a no-win situation and their backs were quite literally against a wall. I can't imagine that anybody, including Moses himself, would have thought a son of Pharaoh would be the one to set them free. God's ways are never our ways and it would do us good to remember that he has a million different strategies to free us from the pits we have fallen into and the prison doors we have locked ourselves behind.

It is interesting to note that in the verse prior to the one quoted above from Psalm 40, David was not asked to give a good reason for being pulled out of the pit. He wasn't required to work harder next time, nor was he evaluated based on his gender, race or financial status. Verse 1 simply says: 'I waited patiently for the LORD; he turned to me and heard my cry.'

Patience

Patience is not only a virtue in the kingdom of God; it is a necessity. Walking by faith and trusting God *wholly* means

I do not hold him ransom to my timetable. Too often we will pray for a miracle, ask for a healing, plead for an intervention, and then get upset when a week or two (or year or two) passes and we have not seen our breakthrough. Are we willing to wait *as long as it takes*? Are we willing to trust that the Bible is true despite our circumstances? There is nowhere in Scripture where we are encouraged to give up, quit or stop believing. Put bluntly: God is not a God of quitting.

Instead, we are told to persevere, hold on to our faith, believe, repeatedly speak to the mountain of difficulty and command it to be cast into the sea. Who are we to introduce limitation to the unlimited one? I am convinced, because of what I have seen in my own life, that the reason many (not all) answers to prayer are not received is because the person stopped believing. Before you write me a nasty letter, I am not saying that we can manipulate God into anything because of our prayers, nor am I saying that it is always our fault (or our sin) that has caused the answer to appear as 'no'. God is too complex and there are too many factors involved to simplify an understanding of the ways of God. He is God and his ways are definitely beyond our ways, and certainly at times beyond our understanding. But I *am* saying that faith is a crucial key to believing and to receiving – we cannot even get saved without faith, so how can we expect any other answer to come without faith?

With that, God must always be our focus and our desire – not the answer to our prayer. We must seek him above all others and desire him above our desire, knowing that his nature is love and his character is goodness. He is not trying to keep things from us – he is trying to get them to us! We see this in Psalm 37:4; Psalm 35:27; Matthew 6:33; Philippians 4:19 . . . and many other scriptures.

To be honest, if we expect the worst we will probably find it. If we keep complaining, we'll only feel more miserable.

But if we choose to worship and put our trust in God, not for what he can give us but simply because we love him for who he is, then everything changes. A wonderful scripture addressing this is 1 Corinthians 10:13 (TPT):

> We all experience times of testing, which is normal for every human being. But God will be faithful to you. He will screen and filter the severity, nature, and timing of every test or trial you face so that you can bear it. And each test is an opportunity to trust him more, for along with every trial God has provided for you a way of escape that will bring you out of it victoriously.

Jerry Bridges posted the following in the online Billy Graham magazine:

> The object of our faith is the person of God Himself; not our faith. When I do not have faith, I'm saying one of two things: either God cannot answer this prayer or God will not answer this prayer. If I say He cannot, I'm questioning His sovereignty and His power. If I say He will not, I'm questioning His goodness. To pray in faith means that I believe God can and I believe God will insofar as it's consistent with His glory, because God is good.[1]

I believe one of the greatest tests of our faith – and what often keeps us distanced from God – is having to wait. Can we believe God is good even when the answer is delayed or he appears absent? Can we continue to declare the truth of what we believe from the Bible, even in the face of facts that speak otherwise? Regularly I hear people say they believe God can heal them, but then they spend 90% of their time talking about their ailment, their pain and how they cannot see a way out of it.

I am not diminishing the pain and am certainly not intending judgment for those who live with chronic pain. I honestly *cannot* imagine how difficult it must be and how challenging it would be to trust for a breakthrough when your body is screaming out the opposite. We are all on a journey and wherever you are in the journey, I sincerely champion you. Even the fact that you are reading this book says a tremendous amount, so please do not misunderstand the heart behind my words. But patience requires us to *act* on what we know, because knowledge alone does not save or heal us, and doubt and fear will always mislead us.

For example, I can know not to eat the chocolate because it has sugar and I'm wanting to cut back, but if I don't act on that knowledge when I'm tempted then knowledge will actually do me no good. I can know that God saves people and Jesus died on the cross for my salvation, but if I don't respond to that knowledge then I am still separated from him for eternity. In the same way, I can know what the Bible says about my situation and that by his stripes I am healed or that he is my provider or that he will never leave me or forsake me, but if I choose not to listen because the facts are tempting me to believe otherwise, then I have nobody to blame but myself. God will not override my will, and my words are a creative force that will lead me either towards wholeness, joy and abundant life, or towards negativity, sarcasm and a life void of peace and joy. Quite simply: negativity and peace cannot co-exist.

> Quite simply: negativity and peace cannot co-exist.

Nowhere in the Bible does God encourage us to have a pessimistic, sarcastic or defeatist attitude and he certainly never soothes anyone into complacency over their doubts, but instead he repeatedly encourages us to rejoice and be thankful. We don't have to be a theologian to know that negative and sarcastic words impact atmospheres for harm and not for good.

Have you ever walked into a room after there has been an argument? Without having heard the conversation you know that hurtful words have just been spoken because you can feel the effect of them lingering in the air. In the same manner, gratefulness, encouragement and thankfulness will change the atmosphere (and circumstances) for good.

Continuing with Psalm 40, we read in verse 3, 'He put a new song in my mouth, a hymn of praise to our God. Many will see and fear the LORD and put their trust in him.' Notice that David spoke something new out of his mouth – not an old song, but a new song. Some of you may need to start singing a new song over an old issue or a broken relationship. Begin listening to yourself: how often do you speak negatively about a person, condition, situation or ailment? What would it look like to change your tune, so to speak?

Imagine if we substituted all our negativity for words of trust, faith and joy – what a different atmosphere we would create in and around our home, let alone our community! I used to complain regularly, and while it was cute when I was 3, it had become a habit by the age of 13. Once I hit 30 and was still living in a cesspool of self-pity . . . well, it had now become caustic.

The difficulty was that I was blinded to the depth of my negativity until I became surrounded by people of faith. In an environment that focuses on possibility and meditates on the truth, self-pity quickly became a stench and I began to notice I smelled . . . terrible!

Faith

Hebrews 11 is the famous 'faith chapter' of the Bible, and included in the line-up of spiritual greats is our friend Moses.

He was a man of faith, and one of the main tenets of faith is that faith is not limited by sight, but trusts in what is unseen. Hebrews 11:1 says: 'Now faith is confidence in what we hope for and assurance about what we do not see.'

We will not walk out of hiding if we remain cemented in unbelief and doubt, because they will – by their very nature – chain us to a weight of facts and reality. Faith lives above reality, because from a spiritual perspective we are seated in heavenly places in Christ Jesus; I do not deny what I see, but I refuse to let what I see dictate my life. It is a simple mindset shift that will transform our spiritual lives if we believe it to be true.

Either God is God or he is not. Either he has conquered sin, death and the grave or he has not. And if he has, then that is where I place my trust and my hope – for all eternity. I am not saying it is easy; in fact, it is much easier to live with an attitude of 'what may be may be' and to hope that something will change, while not really expecting anything to change. That is far easier than standing in faith, believing the word of God over our circumstances, and refusing to let our feelings and facts dictate our emotional state for the day. The power of life and death are in our words – we literally infect our homes, workplaces, communities and hearts with our words, positively or negatively.

> Either God is God or he is not. Either he has conquered sin, death and the grave or he has not.

Imagine if Moses' parents had chosen to complain about the terrible law enacted by Pharaoh, never fighting for his freedom but instead resigning themselves to the will of the evil one. Or what if Moses had stayed in Midian complaining that he had been misunderstood, choosing to wallow in self-pity for the rest of his days? Can you imagine Jesus complaining to the disciples when they forgot the food (I would have!) or complaining to the Pharisees when they refused to believe who he was, or complaining to the disciples who woke him up to quieten the storm *they* were supposed to take responsibility for? It was not in his nature to complain because Hebrews 1:3 says that Jesus is the exact representation of the Father. In other words, if God doesn't complain, then neither does Jesus – and neither should we.

Put bluntly, complaining is cousins with self-pity and is rooted in a self-centred type of behaviour that is not God honouring, revealing a remarkable lack of self-control. Author and speaker John Bevere puts it even more directly:

> Complaining is a killer. It will short-circuit the life of God in you faster than almost any other thing! Complaining indirectly communicates to the Lord, 'I don't like what You are doing in my life – and if I were You, I would do it differently.' Complaining is nothing more than a manifestation of insubordination to God's authority. It is extremely irreverent! God hates it![2]

Philippians 2:14 says: 'Do everything without grumbling or arguing', and in this passage 'everything' means 'each and every part that makes up a whole'. Nothing is missing or left out – everything means . . . everything. There is no room for misinterpretation or justification in that word! God would not ask something of us that was not possible; therefore, it must be possible to live a life without complaint regardless of what we see in our natural circumstances. I am not saying it is easy, but I *am* saying it is biblical.

At the same time, I believe we must be honest with God about how we are really feeling; otherwise we are in danger of stepping into a different aspect of hiding – denial. Pretending we are fine will never set us free, and simply repeating Scripture by rote, with no real belief attached to it, does not impress a God who knows our hearts.

Be honest with him, get angry if need be, and give yourself time to process the confusion and grief. Perhaps you will even visit the campsite of complaint for a season – that's understandable – but reject the temptation to establish a home in that place.

Keep seeking, worshipping, talking, and allowing the Holy Spirit to lead you *through* the valley. On the other side, your faith will eventually loose you from the bonds of cynicism, negativity and self-pity – releasing you from a prison of pain into a place of purpose.

This decision is so important because the journey starts getting exciting now . . . it is time to explore.

For Reflection

- Are there areas in your life where you feel you are behind prison doors? If you knew the door was actually unlocked, would you leave?

- Who are your 'faith friends'?

- Are you a person who gives up easily? If so, what steps could you take to move from quitting to standing?

- 'We will not walk out of hiding if we remain cemented in unbelief and doubt, because they will – by their very nature – chain us to a weight of facts and reality.' Are there any areas in your life that are being weighed down by unbelief and doubt?

Part Three

Exploring

8

Make It Personal

I want to know Christ – yes, to know the power
of his resurrection and participation in his suffer-
ings, becoming like him in his death . . .

                                          Phil. 3:10

I remember at university we created this game where a few
friends and I would write on a piece of paper 'left', 'right',
'straight', 'right', 'left', 'left', 'right' . . . and then after we had
about twenty random directions written down we would drive
to a starting point and follow the piece of paper. We had great
expectations of arriving in another state hours away, going on
a grand adventure and possibly experiencing a new culture –
when in reality we never made it out of town. It was basically a
roadmap that led nowhere, because it never
occurred to us that if we took the first
choice every time we came upon a road, we
would basically go in circles.

Any good explorer knows that if you
want to reach your destination you must
have some type of a map. It may seem that
a good pioneer throws caution to the wind

> Any good
> explorer knows
> that if you want
> to reach your
> destination you
> must have some
> type of a map.

and goes wherever the wind blows them, but doing so subjects them to the wind, not their will.

Equally, a good explorer (or anyone with a vision) always begins from where they are because, without knowing our current location, we cannot navigate to a desired destination. We see this even in a shopping mall – if we want to find a certain place, what do we do? We look at the information screen for the 'You Are Here' star. Once we know where we are standing, it becomes easier to locate the nearest coffee shop (priorities, people).

Like most things in life, people can fall into two extremes when it comes to direction: control freak or passive observer. One tries to manipulate every decision, plan for every eventuality and control every interruption, and the other assumes *que sera sera* and hopes for the best. Neither cultivates peace and both relegate God to the sidelines, hindering our future by a lack of faith.

Carrying on from the last chapter, we see that faith believes, trusts, declares and expects a good outcome. It hears from heaven, walks in obedience and stands against the enemy. It fights for what is right and it won't back down in the face of defeat. Equally, it will not live with entitlement or demand its own way. Its authority is from the word of God and its assurance is from the nature of God. It speaks with confidence, not arrogance, and it expects things based on Bible hope, not self-determination. The only way we can live this type of victorious faith is to have our identity grounded in Christ, and our flesh submitted to our spirit. It is a daily decision and lifetime journey of discovery – intimate, personal and freeing.

So, before we delve into the specific decisions Moses made to reach a face-to-face relationship with God, I want us to pinpoint our spiritual location.

Imagine your relationship with the Lord is like the information map at a shopping centre and God the Father, Jesus and Holy Spirit are sitting at the local Starbucks having a good ol' natter.[1] Where would your spiritual 'You Are Here' star be placed in relation to their location? Would you be walking around searching for them or hiding out in the store furthest away from their known location?

To Know Him

I became a Christian at the age of 19 and I remember falling quickly in love with Jesus, remaining at a safe distance from the Father and pretty much ignoring Holy Spirit. I was afraid of the Father and, quite frankly, thought Holy Spirit was weird – so Jesus was my safe place. One of the greatest joys and journeys of my life has been increasing my knowledge of Jesus and being introduced to the truth of the Father and the joy of Holy Spirit. It seems the more I know about them, the more I feel I don't know!

In the Philippians 3 scripture at the beginning of the chapter, the word 'know' is *ginōskō* in the Greek and it means 'to know through personal experience', as Mary meant when she said that she had not 'known' a man (Luke 1:34).[2] It is an intimate knowing, different from another Greek word (*eidō*) which means knowing by observation.[3] In the Garden of Eden there was complete transparency, vulnerability, nakedness, love, peace, joy and a full *knowing* between God and humanity. It was a Spirit-to-spirit relationship – the glory of the Lord consuming and clothing the atmosphere. I believe that this knowing is what God longs to have with his children once again.

How well do you know the Father, Son, and Holy Spirit? I have had seasons where I was led to know one aspect of the

Trinity in a greater degree, increasing my love for them as a whole throughout the process. At this point, it would do us good to remember that they are three distinct persons, but one Godhead. Each one has a different role and each can play a different part in our love relationship. Without going deep into it theologically, at its most basic the Father is the Creator of all; Jesus is our Saviour and brother – the one who has made an intimate relationship possible once again; and Holy Spirit is with us 24/7 as our counsellor, guide and comforter. Perhaps thinking of them individually will help God seem more approachable, because though they are one, they also are three distinct persons with three distinct roles.

> Though they are one, they also are three distinct persons with three distinct roles.

Therefore, before we go further I want us to pause and examine our relationship with the Father, Son and Holy Spirit, reflecting on our interaction with each one of them.

Father

You may have heard that we often see our earthly father as a type of our heavenly Father. If someone had an earthly father who was harsh and critical, then they may grow up with an image of Father God being disappointed in them and/or angry all the time. Hearing the word 'father' conjures up a plethora of emotions, thoughts, feelings and memories for each one of us. We have all seen incredible examples of a godly father who loved and accepted his children, cheering them on to greatness; as well as those fathers who instilled fear and control, often out of their own sense of pain or insecurity. I would imagine that most fathers fall somewhere in-between the two: doing the best they can and learning to love from a place of vulnerability, amid their own private battles.

It is good to remember that Jesus had no fear of his Father. Even before his ministry started, Jesus felt and heard the approval of heaven through the booming voice at his baptism saying: 'This is my Son, whom I love; with him I am well pleased.'[4]

In John 10:30 Jesus says: 'I and the Father are one.'

And finally in John 5:19: 'Very truly I tell you, the Son can do nothing by himself; he can do only what he sees his Father doing, because whatever the Father does the Son also does.'

How well do you know your heavenly Father? I have a very loving earthly father; I know that he would do anything in his power to keep me from harm and to provide for my needs. He loves to spend time with me, and our once-a-year fishing trip on the lake is one of my most treasured days of the year! Yet, growing up, there were still times when I felt I wasn't good enough for him, that I could have done better and that he was disappointed in me. Much of this was probably my own inse-curity – my sister was a (nearly) 'straight A' student and, though more rebellious than me, she was the one who worked hard and got the great grades. I, on the other hand, enjoyed having an adventure in the woods, cramming to study for a test only be-cause I had to and dreaming of becoming a famous film actress one day. It is little wonder that my father held some sense of concern for my future! There were numerous times of affirma-tion, encouragement, countless cuddles, and endless games of playing together after he arrived home from a long day at work, but I still remember the hurt I felt when I wasn't able to hit the mark and I knew deep down that I had disappointed him.

Learning to receive love from my heavenly Father is a jour-ney I am still walking and one that presumably will carry on into eternity. My experiences do not define him, and if I'm ever in doubt about his love I only need to think of his Son hanging on a cross for my own sins and I have my answer: his love for me (and you) is *immeasurable*.

At the same time, we have all experienced times when we feel God has abandoned or deserted us – those times when he seems a million miles away, no matter how long and hard we pray. There are numerous reasons for his apparent absence (he promises never to leave us or forsake us, so he's never really absent) and, to be honest, it is to our benefit that he doesn't give in to our every wish and whim. I've seen fathers behave like that – they cannot say no to their children, letting the children rule the home instead of the parent. That isn't love; that is born out of their own need and can be deeply damaging to the child in the long run. But our heavenly Father has no lack; and being omniscient and omnipresent he has no need for anyone else, yet without us there would be something missing for him. It's a paradox that I won't try to explain or articulate as it is well beyond my spiritual pay grade!

I do know this: he is love, and because love needs another for the object of its affection, there is a need for companionship . . . even for the creator of the universe.

> He is love, and because love needs another for the object of its affection, there is a need for companionship . . . even for the creator of the universe.

Son

Early in my Christian walk I asked Jesus to teach me what it would look like for a man to love me in a healthy way. Due to past experiences with boys when I was younger, I knew that fear was the foundation under which I saw romantic relationships – and

I also knew this was not how I wanted to live the rest of my life. So one day I decided that I would try to build a trusting love relationship with Jesus, as I would if I had a husband. It started one evening when I thought to myself: *What would I do if I were newly married and my husband was coming home from work?*

I am very affected by atmosphere so I knew the first thing I wanted to do was to create a beautiful ambience in the house. Growing up, my sister and I had to cook the family meal a few times a month and we could make whatever we wanted; it was completely our choice and responsibility. My sister created amazing meals, following the recipe down to the letter.

I, on the other hand, created great ambience.

Lowering the lights, I would choose the perfect candles, put on lovely music . . . and then make something out of a box. My food left quite a bit to be desired, but the atmosphere was brilliant!

Now, back to Jesus: I began practising 'how to love' by lowering the lights, putting on jazz music, lighting the candles, making a sandwich, and then I would stare at the empty chair I set out for him and . . . hesitantly (awkwardly) ask Jesus about his day. I waited a few minutes, but . . . heard nothing (I think I would have fainted outright if he had actually answered me). Since he was silent, I proceeded telling him about my day.

Then, after a few minutes of strained one-sided conversation, I tried helping things along by offering him talking points: had he healed anyone that day? Performed many miracles? Averted disasters overseas? Finally, I laughed at my crazy imagination and finished my sandwich while reading a book.

But something had shifted in my heart.

There was a warmth and sense of closeness that hadn't been present before we sat down to dinner. It was then that I knew the truth of the scripture: if we draw near to him, he will draw near to us.[5] So began my journey of drawing near. I would talk to Jesus as I was driving in the car, hold his hand as I walked down the road, imagine him running with me (his hair always in a ponytail) when I was out jogging . . . Jesus simply became a part of my everyday life.

Spirit

It was my first experience with a charismatic church. To say I was hesitant is a remarkable understatement – terrified would be more appropriate. I had been 'warned off' Holy Spirit meetings and up to now had steered well clear of anything I couldn't control. But for some reason I decided to attend this particular meeting . . . and I will never forget it.

Most of the service is a blur, but the offering time is crystal clear in my memory. Now, let me be clear: I am passionate about giving and generosity and I believe God is extremely interested in our finances, for the right reasons. He is a God of abundance and he has no problem giving extravagantly (he gave his only Son), but he also expects us to walk in wisdom with our finances and to listen to him about how to steward them and where to sow. Giving generously can be a blessing to others, but if it's given with the wrong motive, or for self-promotion, then it will not be blessed.

So, here I was in what can only be described as complete chaos. There was absolutely no order to the service, people were running wild, there were loud and strange noises everywhere, and I was absolutely paralysed with fear and confusion. (Note: I've been part of charismatic churches for years and I have never come across anything like this since that time.) For the offering, the pastor explained that whoever gave 10% of their current debt total into this offering would see their debt completely cleared by God within the next few months. I couldn't believe my ears! I had debt from (paying for) university which I had diligently been trying to pay off for years, and seemingly not making much headway. If this was the truth, then I was in!

(In case it wasn't clear – that pastor's claim is *not* truth.)

I wrote a cheque and eagerly joined the queue of people bringing their 'debt-breaking offering' to the front. Once I got to the front I placed it in the basket and turned around to leave. That's when I realized I was trapped. The people behind me began to sway, pray, dance, twirl, and even convulse on the floor in front of me. I was petrified. This was my first real experience with the Holy Spirit in action and, I must say, it was not pleasant.

Perhaps you can relate? Maybe, like me, you have kept Holy Spirit at a distance because of misunderstanding, fear, misrepresentation or as a result of doctrinal teaching. Sadly there has been an enormous amount of misunderstanding, criticism and mocking of the Third Person of the Trinity, and though I would not be so presumptuous as to say I fully understand him, I have learned that he is not who I thought he was. What was represented that evening was far from the Holy Spirit I know and love today; the congregation had allowed their emotions to take control and soon the flesh was in control, not the spirit.

A few years after the event, I asked Holy Spirit to reveal himself to me . . . gently. He knew my fears, and if there is one thing I have learned about him, it is this: he is a perfect gentleman. He will never push you beyond where you want to go, yet he is happy to lead you further than you have been before.

> He will never push you beyond where you want to go, yet he is happy to lead you further than you have been before.

Three in One

Coming out of hiddenness will only happen if we trust God's holiness. Trusting his holiness will only happen as we know his character. His character will only be fully known as we meet him as Father, Son *and* Holy Spirit – three in one.

Which one of the Godhead are you most comfortable with? Recently I challenged someone in this area and I was thrilled to speak to her a few weeks later and hear about her experience. She said that she had always pictured God as personal, yet 'big' and far away. One morning she chose to invite Jesus into her lounge; she imagined him sitting with her and then she asked what he wanted to say. She went on to explain that she had the most powerful experience with him that morning, forever changing her relationship with him.

Now – back to the shopping mall.

Take some time to imagine yourself walking nearer to that coffee shop; can you see them chatting together in joy, peace and perfect love?

Notice the empty chair at the table?

That's for you.

For Reflection

- Where would your 'You Are Here' star be placed in relation to your relationship with the Father, Son and Holy Spirit?

- Which one of the Godhead are you most comfortable with? Why do you think that is?

- When have you felt closest to: Father, Son, and/or Holy Spirit?

- Do you have any questions about the nature or character of the persons of the Trinity? (If you are doing this as a group, share your answer with your group leader.) The Bible says in Jeremiah 29:13 that as we seek God, we will find him. We cannot ever *fully* understand him, but we are meant to enjoy the journey getting to know him.

9

What a Difference a Day Makes

'Do not come any closer,' God said. 'Take off your sandals, for the place where you are standing is holy ground.'

Exod. 3:5

For my parents' fiftieth wedding anniversary we bought them a large picture which says 'What a Difference a Day Makes' across the top and then underneath it lists their wedding date, the birthdates of their children and their fiftieth wedding anniversary date. It hangs in their lounge as a beautiful reminder that one day can – literally – change everything.

There are people in my life right now who are extremely significant to me, yet the day that I met them was an ordinary day like any other. I could not have known the impact their friendship or relationship would have in my life because the initial day(s) was so ordinary. It makes me think back to my move to England. God clearly called me to this marvellous island, but not knowing anyone meant it wasn't an option to get a work visa before arriving. Logically it seemed wise to remain in America until I had sorted the visa, but after praying about it I knew God was saying to leave, and trust him for the details.

It reminded me of God's word to Abraham: leave and then I will show you what to do. So, not long after that, I landed at Heathrow airport not knowing how I would get permission to stay, but knowing that I was clearly called.

I applied for a visa after arriving, and four months later – much to my horror – it was denied. Having quit my job, sold my home, given away my possessions and left all earthly security to move across the Atlantic . . . I was now being told I had to return to America. On the advice of my pastor I approached my local MP[1] for advice.

His advice? Go home.

I assured him that I would leave . . . but that I would also return. My faith was severely tested in the few weeks that I went back to the States – common sense telling me to let the dream go, the Chicago Passport Agency refusing to release my passport because they 'didn't think I looked like a pastor', and even some close friends and family members wondering if I had completely lost the plot. But I knew what God had said. So, by faith, I booked a return flight for two weeks later, and two days before I was due to fly my passport was finally released – I was free to return to England.

I wrote a note to the local MP letting him know they had let me back into the country, and a few weeks later I heard his bellowing voice in the church office asking, 'Where is that Jennifer girl?'

Ummm . . . that would be me, sir.

He couldn't figure out how this female pastor was allowed back into the country because, in his words, England didn't need me. (Gee, thanks.)

I told him it was because God wanted me here.

'It can't be God,' he said.

'It was God,' I replied.

'It can't be God,' he said again.

'It was God,' I replied again.

With a slight grunt of annoyance he said, 'Well . . . if you are going to live in our country, then you need to know how to make a decent cup of tea. Follow me.'

And thus began our journey together – one which would see him becoming a bit of a grandfather figure, inviting me to the Houses of Parliament, dragging me before Boris Johnson because 'you really must meet him', inviting me to tea with the President of Brazil and continually telling me to 'get a real job' (because ministry clearly was not one).

He also invited me to 10 Downing Street, at the invitation of the Prime Minister, to an Anti-Trafficking Day celebration. It was there my season of work in the anti-trafficking field began.

I never could have imagined that one conversation about a denied visa would open doors that literally changed the trajectory of my life. I'm sure you also have stories in your own life of people who have made a significant difference after an insignificant beginning. Trusting God in the everyday moments of life is critical if we want to live a life of faith, because the moments we see as ordinary are the very ones he transforms to extraordinary. But if we are trying to control every little decision and eventuality in our lives, we will miss some of the most stunning relationships and twists and turns that life can bring us.

> The moments we see as ordinary are the very ones he transforms to extraordinary.

Let's now return to Moses and explore the key steps necessary for a face-to-face relationship with the Lord. It all began with an ordinary bush . . . that was not so ordinary.

Just Your Average Day

Growing up in Pharaoh's household, Moses must have known that he was adopted. Somewhere during his growing-up years he also probably learned of Pharaoh's decision to murder all Hebrew boys his age, which may well have skewed how he saw his adopted family. Perhaps he was thankful for the rich up-bringing and favour on his life, yet guilt-ridden over those who did not have the same fortune as himself? Maybe he wondered why his life was spared, leaving him feeling a sense of debt that he needed to repay to the Israelites?

Whatever the reason for Moses' streak of justice – whether inborn or experience driven – it sealed his fate as an exile for the majority of his adult life. An exile who eventually found his home in perfect love, not perfect surroundings. But before we go there, let's remind ourselves of one very significant day in Moses' life:

> Now Moses was tending the flock of Jethro his father-in-law, the priest of Midian, and he led the flock to the far side of the wilderness and came to Horeb, the mountain of God. There the angel of the LORD appeared to him in flames of fire from within a bush. Moses saw that though the bush was on fire it did not burn up. So Moses thought, 'I will go over and see this strange sight – why the bush does not burn up.'
>
> When the LORD saw that he had gone over to look, God called to him from within the bush, 'Moses! Moses!'
>
> And Moses said, 'Here I am.'
>
> 'Do not come any closer,' God said. 'Take off your sandals, for the place where you are standing is holy ground.' Then he said, 'I am the God of your father, the God of Abraham, the God of

Isaac and the God of Jacob.' At this, Moses *hid his face*, because he was afraid to look at God.

The LORD said, 'I have indeed seen the misery of my people in Egypt. I have heard them crying out because of their slave drivers, and I am concerned about their suffering. So I have come down to rescue them from the hand of the Egyptians and to bring them up out of that land into a good and spacious land, a land flowing with milk and honey – the home of the Canaanites, Hittites, Amorites, Perizzites, Hivites and Jebusites. And now the cry of the Israelites has reached me, and I have seen the way the Egyptians are oppressing them. So now, go. I am sending you to Pharaoh to bring my people the Israelites out of Egypt.'[2]

Moses was going about his day-to-day activity, tending the sheep, when God intervened. He could not have known that all his years tending sheep were training for tending a nation, but God knew. He is always watching, teaching, preparing. We must never – ever – think our daily lives, however insignificant they seem at the moment, are unrelated to the greater purpose of our lives. When we are obediently walking, God is strategically leading.

> When we are obediently walking, God is strategically leading.

Notice where Moses was when he received his next assignment: the far side of the wilderness. If we long for greater holiness, we *must* learn to embrace the wilderness. It is often in the dark places, when God seems out of reach, that we are being shaped and moulded for our next season. Without the unpretentious wilderness, Moses might never have seen the Promised Land.

A Burning Bush

A burning bush wasn't unusual in the desert. Foliage often caught fire from the heat and burned to the ground, usually limiting the damage to a shrub and nothing more. This particular bush was most likely a thorn-bush, the most insignificant bush of that time.[3] That is where the insignificance ends, because anything God's glory touches leaves an impression that cannot be ignored. Moses had no idea he was about to encounter God, or that the rest of his life would literally never look the same; he simply knew that his Tuesday suddenly became more interesting. (It probably wasn't a Tuesday, but I like to think that it was.) Regardless, it was the ordinary suddenly made extraordinary.

Moses had not been actively searching for a new vocation, nor were God-sightings in local bushes the norm in those days. In fact, it is helpful to remember that there weren't any appearances (recorded in Scripture) of God to *anyone* since Jacob a few hundred years prior to this. In our New Testament world, when people can hear from the Lord on a regular basis, that can be difficult to comprehend. Imagine going your entire life and never encountering God's presence; in fact, not knowing a single person who had experienced an encounter with God for several *generations*. We can be fairly confident that meeting God in a bush was not on Moses' list of goals for the year, but God has a wonderful way of tracking us down wherever we place our feet.

> God has a wonderful way of tracking us down wherever we place our feet.

It is also helpful to remember that when he calls, we must be ready to answer – because he calls, he does not coerce. When we surrender our lives to the Lord, walking in obedience without requiring an explanation, we will inevitably see doors open that seem unusual at the moment, yet providential in hindsight. But if we insist on being in control, God will never force what we won't allow. Though far more challenging, I find Moses' way a great deal more interesting.

So Moses saunters over to the bush to see what has not been seen before – the angel of the Lord[4] calling to him. Moses replies 'Here I am' and God quickly reminds him that unholy sandals are not meant to tread on holy ground. (Have you ever been to someone's house and after you enter they look at your feet rather than your face . . . hint. It was a bit like that, but to a holy extreme.) In ancient Egyptian times, and in eastern countries today, shoes are removed as a sign of respect, but also as an admittance of 'unworthiness' to stand in front of holiness. The shoes were caked in dust, dirt, excrement and anything else that felt like hitching a ride through the far side of the wilderness – none of which was appropriate before the purest purity that exists. It reminds me of Jesus' blood, which allows me to approach a holy God, in whatever state I am in, because I am seen washed in the blood of Jesus and not covered in the stain of my sin. In this instance it was holiness – not tidiness – that was of concern to God.

Once the shoes were removed, Moses' journey towards holiness could truly begin.

Promotion

Any promotion can be daunting, but I think promotion in the kingdom of God is especially disconcerting because it will always require our dependence on the Lord to do the job he's asking us to do. Peter's promotion went from fisherman to main stage-speaker, Joseph was promoted from prisoner to Prime Minister, and precious Mary goes from virgin to mother of Jesus – promotion in the kingdom is always well outside our abilities and comfort zone. Once we accept this truth, the quicker we can release control and the easier it will be for the Lord to strategically move us within his plans and purposes for our lives.

The Bible says in Zechariah 4:10 not to despise the days of small beginnings and I think that is in part so we grow in confidence during the 'behind the scenes' days. That is the time God is preparing, pruning and perfecting us for the next season. If we bemoan our days of walking we will never learn to run. I am not a professional athlete (that was the understatement of the year) but I do know that the basics are what brings out the brilliance. A good individual or team will rehearse the basics *repeatedly* because it is the basic skills that consistently win games, not the 'lucky' plays. There is no substitute for practice, hard work and diligence – in sport or in life!

Is there anything in your life that represents 'shoes' needing to be removed? Something that might get in the way of your ability to converse with the Lord undistracted and unhindered?

> It is impossible to touch his presence and not have his presence touch you.

Quite simply: *it is impossible to touch his presence and not have his presence touch you.*

To move forward, we must answer the question: am I willing to be diligent today in preparation for promotion tomorrow?

Moses may have removed his shoes, but as we will see, he still had much to learn.

For Reflection

- What are some significant dates in your own life, when you knew things would never be the same? How does that make you feel – sorrowful or joyful, or both?

- How do you think Moses felt on the day he realized the murder was public knowledge and he would have to leave Egypt?

- What does holiness mean to you? How do you symbolically 'remove your shoes' in the presence of God?

- Do you enjoy or fear promotion?

10

Resistance and Roadblocks

But I know that the king of Egypt will not let you go unless a mighty hand compels him. So I will stretch out my hand and strike the Egyptians with all the wonders that I will perform among them. After that, he will let you go.

Exod. 3:19–20

Have you ever been in the middle of an argument you were losing – and consequently, one in which you knew you were wrong – yet you still refused to give up the fight?

No, me neither.

But I have heard there are people like that.

Moses found himself having a bit of a tussle with the Lord which, let's be honest, does not make him the brightest bulb in the bunch. As if God is suddenly going to say, 'Oh, you're right – I hadn't thought of that. I'm so sorry, my mistake.'

It's not going to happen.

Before we delve further into examining their conversation – or discussion – or let's be honest: *the Lord listening to Moses complain* – let's remind ourselves of what happened in Exodus 4:1–9:

Moses answered, 'What if they do not believe me or listen to me and say, "The Lord did not appear to you"?'

Then the LORD said to him, 'What is that in your hand?'

'A staff,' he replied.

The LORD said, 'Throw it on the ground.'

Moses threw it on the ground and it became a snake, and he ran from it. Then the LORD said to him, 'Reach out your hand and take it by the tail.' So Moses reached out and took hold of the snake and it turned back into a staff in his hand. 'This,' said the LORD, 'is so that they may believe that the LORD, the God of their fathers – the God of Abraham, the God of Isaac and the God of Jacob – has appeared to you.'

Then the LORD said, 'Put your hand inside your cloak.' So Moses put his hand into his cloak, and when he took it out, the skin was leprous – it had become as white as snow.

'Now put it back into your cloak,' he said. So Moses put his hand back into his cloak, and when he took it out, it was restored, like the rest of his flesh.

Then the LORD said, 'If they do not believe you or pay attention to the first sign, they may believe the second. But if they do not believe these two signs or listen to you, take some water from the Nile and pour it on the dry ground. The water you take from the river will become blood on the ground.'

Moses' insecurity reared its ugly head moments after he was promoted from shepherding sheep to leading a nation (admittedly, quite a jump).

In Exodus 3:21–22 God told Moses: 'And I will make the Egyptians favourably disposed towards this people, so that when you leave you will not go empty-handed. Every woman is to ask her neighbour and any woman living in her house for articles of silver and gold and for clothing, which you will put on your sons and daughters. And so you will plunder the Egyptians.'

Moses had just learned that not only was he being promoted to a new (major) assignment, but also his financial status was going to significantly rise. This is good news, people. Imagine if God appeared to you and said that he had a little assignment for you that was going to take you far beyond your comfort zone, but not to worry as he would be with you, and that you would start off with a million pounds[1] being deposited into your chosen bank account.

I am not saying that finances are the only reason to do something or that God was using them as bait to his plan – he was not, because he is not manipulative – but I am saying that blessing (which literally means 'being empowered to prosper') was declared over Moses before he even had time to squeeze out his first excuse. God had promised Moses success, provision and opportunity . . . yet all Moses could see was his inadequacy. Isn't that often the way?

God has plans for us beyond what we could dream or imagine – with provision, favour and blessing promised all throughout the Bible – yet we often limit his plans due to our insecurity, fear or lack of trust in his ability. Imagine what God could do through us if we (unreservedly) trusted him today!

> Imagine what God could do through us if we (unreservedly) trusted him today!

What has he already given you to use for your current assignment – as a mother, business leader, spouse, educator, small-group leader, plumber, pastor, grandparent, volunteer . . .?

We often have more than we realize: eyesight, hearing, shelter, food, mobility, a healthy mind, safe working environment, provision, support . . . and the list could go on. Even if we aren't currently living our best life, we still have copious blessings every minute of every day. If you doubt that, breathe.

You've just been blessed.

Who Is the Hero?

We see in Acts 7:22 (ESV) that Moses was 'mighty in his words and deeds' during his growing-up years. Confidence clearly wasn't an issue for him at one time, yet through the circumstances of life his confidence had become weakened. Therefore, in Exodus 3:11 we hear Moses asking: 'Who am I, to take on this responsibility?' (my paraphrase). One season of life can have us strong in confidence, but one experience in life can shake that confidence to its very core.

Perhaps you have had a similar thought as you held your newborn, looked at your new house, received a work promotion or were invited to lead a ministry team: *Surely I am not ready for this? I've made horrible mistakes in my past; how will I be seen beyond my reputation?* I love how God answered the insecurity of Moses: I will be with you.

In other words, this isn't about you, Moses.

Donald Miller of the business *Building a StoryBrand* explains that the customer, not the business, is always the hero of the story.[2] The premise being that successful marketing shows the customer how they will benefit; it doesn't emphasize the greatness of the business itself. This is because people want stories to be about them – they want to be the hero. As he explains, it is Yoda to Luke in *Star Wars* or Haymitch to Katniss in *The Hunger Games*. They are the guide behind the scenes who allows the upfront character, who often has a weakness they are trying to overcome, realize their potential and win the day. Moses looks like he is the hero in this story, but the true 'hero' is the one who refuses to let him be ordinary.

The first key towards coming out of hiddenness is acknowledging that someone needs what we are carrying.

> The first key toward coming out of hiddenness is acknowledging that someone needs what we are carrying.

Our role is not to be the hero, but to help someone else become all that God has created them to be. It is what God did with us, through his Son. As we are made in his image, that is the legacy that we are all created to work out in our own lives. For Moses, the choice to stop hiding was ultimately fuelled by the revelation that someone needed what he carried and that he indeed was to be the ruler and redeemer of God's people.[3]

Becoming a parent isn't solely about fulfilling maternal or paternal desire, but is also about partnering with God in providing a safe and secure start for this new life to flourish in their own destiny and purpose. Being blessed with a new home isn't about showing off our dream house as much as it is asking God how we can use this space to further his kingdom.

This past year I had a truly miraculous answer to prayer for housing. Since giving up my house and moving to England fifteen years ago, the Lord has always been tremendously faithful to me where housing is concerned. In fact, every place I have lived these past fifteen years has a 'God story' attached to it, but this last one takes the cake! It is too long of a story to explain in detail, but in essence I had been living in temporary accommodation after having moved to Bath several months prior. For several reasons it wasn't feasible in the long term and, having been 'homeless' (living out of suitcases) for several months, I was looking forward to settling down. The problem was that I live 100% by faith and there wasn't enough known income every month to pay rent (at that time I was only covering utilities). Several times God confirmed to me that the housing 'was taken care of', but I didn't know what that meant or when it would get resolved. It is one thing to believe all will be well and it is another to wait several months – or years – for the manifestation of that provision!

Finally, the landlord decided the house needed selling and asked if a few months would be enough time for me to find alternative arrangements. I assured him that was fine . . . and began expecting a miracle. As the weeks went on, it became obvious that there was no way forward in the natural realm and, to make an extremely long story short, a few weeks before needing to move I found myself preaching in America – uncertain where I would sleep a week after my return. I kept declaring: 'God has for me a beautiful home with large windows, lots of light, an office, high ceilings and . . . a dishwasher!' That is what I felt he had put on my heart to believe for as I prayed, and so that is what I was standing in faith to see come to pass. I was prepared to put things in storage if that was how I felt him leading, but up to that point I had no peace about that decision. Being led by peace, not practicality, is absolutely vital in a walk of faith; otherwise we will respond in fear and potentially block the miracle gift that God is preparing for us.

Returning from America I met with the landlord who informed me that 'the strangest thing happened' while I was away: although the house wasn't on the market, someone had offered to pay (nearly all) cash for it. The buyer wasn't in a rush and preferred to wait a while, so would it be OK for me to stay another month? In a word: yes! I was still in the same position as I had been (unable to pay rent) but I knew that God was working behind the scenes and I remained expectant to see how he would work this one out in the next month.

As it turned out, God only needed a few hours.

About two hours after the landlord left, I received a message from someone I had mentored over twenty years prior to this, who had no knowledge of these conversations or dilemma, saying that the Lord had put on her heart to substantially support my ministry by covering a good portion of my rent for an unlimited period of time – did I need that?

Yet again, in a word: yes!

As I write this I am living in a beautiful area of Bath, looking out of sash windows in my office with high ceilings . . . having emptied my dishwasher not too long ago. The reason I share this is first to say: God is faithful! I am so glad I didn't intervene and try to work it out logically. And second, I started praying for my neighbours as soon as I arrived. I am aware that this isn't solely about providing Jen with a beautiful home and a sanctuary from which to work and minister, but it's about the lives of those around me and the tremendous love God has for them.

It is never – ever – solely about us or our dreams. To think otherwise severely limits our potential and surely lessens God's plans. Can we let go long enough to trust him for a bigger picture?

> Can we let go long enough to trust him for a bigger picture?

Pharaoh's Fight

Most of us are familiar with the story of Pharaoh and the ten plagues. Moses has now been away from Egypt for forty years and presumably is not familiar with the current leader (Pharaoh was a title, not a name) whom he is approaching to release the Hebrew slaves from captivity. About seventy families arrived in Egypt at the time of Moses and now they have grown to an estimated (conservatively) 2.5 to 3 million Israelites awaiting their freedom. Moses was a simple shepherd standing against the most powerful man on the planet; it was that generation's 'David and Goliath' moment.

Space does not allow us to closely examine all the plagues and roadblocks put before Moses, but suffice to say that each victory brought yet another challenge: starting with the rivers turning to blood and progressing through frogs, boils and a multitude of other trials. Pharaoh was losing, but he would not quit. It does us good to remember that praying boldly a few times in faith does not mean the enemy will throw in the towel of defeat and scramble away bruised and beaten. He knows that in our flesh we can easily quit, give in and relinquish the seed of the truth for the fruit of a lie. We saw it in Adam and Eve – the enemy does not play fair, always waiting for an opportune moment.

To remain faithful in the fight takes perseverance, determination, belief and grit to outlast one who has been fighting for thousands of years. He is a defeated foe, but he is also a determined fighter. One of the areas we as Christians (especially in the western world) are lacking is in our ability to 'stand and, having done all, stand' (see Eph. 6:13). However things look in your life right now, if God has not said it is finished, then it is not finished. The facts are merely facts; they are not truth. God has never been, and never will be, intimidated or distracted by facts.

His Son was dead – fact. Jesus conquered death – truth.

Never let the facts get in the way of truth.

As Moses pushed through the roadblocks, one after another, things went from bad to worse. Pharaoh increased the burden on the Hebrews by demanding they gather

> Never let the facts get in the way of truth.

their own straw, as well as make the same amount of bricks for their daily quota, which did not endear the Hebrews to their new 'saviour'. So now he had an annoyed Pharaoh and an enraged nation, all wishing he were gone. It usually gets worse before the breakthrough . . . and for Moses, this was only the beginning.

If you are in the same boat, don't despair – blessing is always found on the other side of the battle, if we refuse to quit.

Human Resistance

I'll say it again: an encounter with God is often followed by resistance from people. We must not expect others to celebrate our calling, or even fully understand it. God may provide a few people who are supportive, but there will be others who may think we're way off track and not hearing from the Lord at all.

It is important to listen to our spiritual leaders, as they are there to give guidance and wisdom, yet it is equally important to listen to the still, small voice of God on the inside of us. God will not give our calling to someone else – it is ours. That is what makes a calling difficult at times; we can feel alone and isolated, and the line between assurance and unbelief becomes narrower and narrower. At the end of the day we will stand accountable before God for how we have responded; he knows if our decisions were made in haste, out of pride or from a sincere desire to please him. There is no hiding with God and it is good to remember that the heart is deceptive above all things.[4]

I remember when I knew God was calling me to move to England. Outwardly it looked ludicrous: I had just bought a new house, I had an excellent job at a large church, I was putting money into stocks and a pension, and my family all lived fairly near to me. Moving over 4,000 miles away meant giving all of this up for a future that was completely unknown, in a country that didn't want me, as a single woman in my early thirties.

My senior pastor at the time was reluctant to say the least. He was not opposed; he simply didn't understand. But what was so beautiful, and true to the kingdom, about his response was that there was no attempt to control me or talk me out of my decision. He was honest enough to say that he couldn't understand why I wanted to do this – and to ask if I had really thought this through properly – but at the end of the day he gave his blessing and honoured me for my years serving in Grand Rapids, Michigan. I will forever be grateful for his godly response.

Fast-forward fifteen years and I can clearly see the hand of God in the move. I truly cannot imagine who I would have become if I had not obeyed the leading of God – as crazy as it looked at the time.

What represents Pharaoh in your life today? Are there road-blocks keeping you from smoothly transitioning into something new? Roadblocks will either draw us nearer in relationship with the Lord, or force us further from his plans, purposes and (potentially) presence.

As always, the choice is ours: give in to the challenge or per-severe through the pain.

For Reflection

• Moses was promised wealth and success, yet he still was in fear. As a Christian, in what ways can you relate to this?

• Are you often the hero in your own story?

• In what ways are you using God's blessings to bless others and further the kingdom?

• Do you find it easy to listen to the 'still, small voice' on the inside of you (your gut)? What has happened when you have not listened to it?

11

The Reward of Risk

See, I am doing a new thing! Now it springs up;
do you not perceive it? I am making a way in the
wilderness and streams in the wasteland.

Isa. 43:19

We were halfway through our trip, flying from England to India, when disaster struck at 30,000 feet.

The first flight to Dubai had finished, and after a fairly uneventful midnight layover we boarded our next flight to Hyderabad. Finding our seats we buckled up, passed the time a bit chatting, and as it was now about 2 a.m. I pulled on an eye-mask, hoping to catch a bit of sleep.

Suddenly, without warning, I could feel my stomach churning, my temperature soaring and my sight dizzying – this was not good. Waking Lisa, who often travels with me, I demanded she find a sick bag *now*! As she was also half asleep, I knew I would never make it in time. I jumped up, shoved past her and Kim (another member of our team) and literally ran for the tiny cubicle they call a toilet on these planes. About this time I could feel myself wanting to black out, but the girls had followed me and Kim had been trained as a nurse, so she took charge.

What happened next can only be described as a small taste of what hell might feel like. I was sitting on a disgusting floor filled with more germs than a high-school boys' lavatory, literally hugging and hanging my head over a toilet which had been used and sat on by a hundred strangers in the past few hours. I was desperate to pass out, boiling hot, yet unable to move what was churning in my stomach. I overheard the flight attendant tell the ladies they had oxygen. The only thing I wanted at that moment was to be on the ground.

Knowing there was no (safe) way out of that tin can was one of the scariest moments of my life. If it turned into something worse, I knew that reaching a hospital would be futile. I begged God to help me and did everything I could to stay 'in the zone' and not pass out. After what felt like hours . . . well, I'll spare you the details, but let's say things returned to normal. I felt as if I'd been run over by a truck, but I was safe, alive and fully functioning again.

Standing before Pharaoh, Moses could not see a way out of this situation that didn't involve risk; he had to trust God's word. In the natural realm it looked as if God was setting him up to reap what he had sown forty years prior: death. It was walking into the lions' den as fresh meat to a starving cat – he was not coming out of this alive.

To say he must have been afraid would be an understatement, but one thing I have learned in life is this: fear is powerless when faith and favour are in the room.

> Fear is powerless when faith and favour are in the room.

Favour

Surely, LORD, you bless the righteous; you surround them with your favour as with a shield.

Ps. 5:12

For the LORD God is a sun and shield; the LORD
bestows favour and honour; no good thing does he
withhold from those whose way of life is blameless.
                                              Ps. 84:11

Favour belongs to us as children of God; we do not earn it,
nor can we take credit for it – it is a gift from a loving Father
to all who walk in righteousness and are open to receiving it.
My favourite version of Psalm 84:11 is found in the Amplified
Bible (AMPC): 'For the Lord God is a Sun and Shield; the Lord
bestows [present] grace and favor and [future] glory (honor,
splendor, and heavenly bliss)! No good thing will He withhold
from those who walk uprightly.'

Present favour and future glory – it doesn't get much better
than that! For many years I lived as a Christian not recogniz-
ing (or looking for) the favour of God; and we know that we
will find what we seek. If I'm not looking for and expecting
any favour, then I may experience it periodically, but I will not
experience it as a regular part of my relationship with God.
But once I started looking for it, expecting it and even asking
God for it (shock and horror!), I began seeing it all around
my life.

Why is it that we, myself included, feel guilty for being
blessed by God? As if we have done something wrong and
we should apologize for the fact that God is pleased with us?
Sometimes we act as if asking for a blessing from God might
diminish his supply for someone else. Let me be clear: God has
plenty of blessing to go around!

Not only that – he is a loving Father who desires to give
good gifts to his children. To expect him to be anything other
than that is to paint him in a wrong light. Satan is the one who
comes to steal, kill and destroy; it is Jesus who gives life and

gives it to us in abundance, *until it overflows*[1] – that sounds like favour to me.

When Moses took a step of faith and faced off the road-blocks of Pharaoh, the Israelites, and his own insecurities, he was blessed with a favour that released abundance and provision for the next season. Remember how we saw in the previous chapter that in Exodus 3:21–22 the Hebrew women were encouraged to ask their Egyptian neighbours for silver, gold and clothing? God wanted his children to have plenty and for the enemy to be left impoverished, because there is no lack in heaven's economy. I find it fascinating that the Bible says the Egyptians were 'favourably disposed' to let go of their treasures. The root for 'favour' here 'supremely refers to the Lord's favor leaning towards people out of His kind disposition to bless them'.[2]

God's kindness cannot help itself; it is disposed to giving favour and blessing. If he is disposed to giving, then shouldn't we be inclined to receiving? Surely he would expect us to receive what he longs to give? What parent gets excited to give a gift to their child for Christmas, hoping that the son or daughter will turn around and say, 'No thanks, Mum, I'd rather not have a gift this Christmas.' (Words never spoken by a child!)

> God's kindness cannot help itself; it is disposed to giving favour and blessing.

God's kindness favours us through gifts, conversations, relationships, unexpected surprises and a multitude of other ways, because kindness *is* generosity. It is in the very nature of the word itself; it must express itself somehow and, by giving itself away, it is demonstrating an unselfish, unconditional love. The Bible says that the kindness of God leads us to repentance;[3] if that is not generosity, then I don't know what is. Yet we all know that today millions of people are rejecting that very kindness – that favour – being shown them by a Father they are unaware loves them in spite of their sin. I can understand an unbeliever refusing kindness, but a child of God refusing it . . . Seen in that light, it seems naive at best and prideful at worst.

If Only

Recently, I read a social media post that showed a couple in the final months of pregnancy, about to receive their first child into the world. The wife was writing about how she and her husband had sat until the early hours of the morning talking about how their life was going to change very soon and thinking back to all the 'coincidences' that took place in order for them to arrive at this point. There were numerous reasons why they 'shouldn't' have met, got married, developed a strong marriage, been successful in business, or even become pregnant. The odds had been against them in numerous ways, but one thing this woman did again and again was take a chance.

She said yes.

Yes to the flirting, yes to the date, yes to the friendship, yes to the inkling to buy a camera, yes to the risk of dating after being friends for ten years, yes to the marriage, yes to the career change, yes to the IVF after two miscarriages, yes, yes, yes. Each 'yes' took them further and further into a life greater than they could have imagined. She finished by saying that she is convinced there is a God, after seeing the hand of providence and divine interruptions happen over and over again. I would love to meet her one day and share with her more about this God she knows is watching out for her.

But it got me thinking: *How often do I say yes? Am I quick to say yes or quicker to say no?* Has saying 'yes' brought good into your life? What paths have opened up before you and how have you changed because you walked in boldness where others balked in weakness?

Hiddenness will never discover new doors.

We see in the book of Ruth that taking a risk wrote Ruth into the history books. A non-Jewish Moabite was an unlikely candidate to become the great-grandmother of King David, yet one never knows what is on the other side of risk. Several times I have heard about studies with those who are elderly and close to death, asking them about their greatest regrets. They haven't wished for more money or a cleaner house, but often the regret is about not having dared to chase their dreams – they wish they had risked more and feared less. I believe fear has stolen far more dreams than failure ever will, because embracing fear removes the option of failure. And, as any Olympic champion knows, if we can't risk failure, we will never experience reward.

> If we can't risk failure, we will never experience reward.

Imagine if David had let fear talk him out of fighting Goliath, or if Abraham had refused to leave the comfort of his posh existence, or if Jesus hadn't been convinced he could succeed as a human. We think it's a ludicrous thought because we know the end of the stories – they didn't.

I believe the second key in coming out of hiddenness, after acknowledging there is someone out there who needs what we have, is to acknowledge there will be risk involved.

> The second key in coming out of hiddenness . . . is to acknowledge there will be risk involved.

Whether that is drawing closer to the Lord, embarking on a new adventure, becoming vulnerable in a relationship or believing God for a miracle . . . we need to step out to show up.

Give It Up

Have you ever been held up at gunpoint?

Me neither.

But I know a few people who have, and it was not a pleasant experience, to put it mildly. They were completely helpless, vulnerable, unarmed, frightened, and at a complete and total disadvantage – subject to the whim of the enemy. All survived miraculously, and new paths have been forged and people helped as a result: God always has the final word.

Risk begins with our mindset – how we view ourselves in the light of our identity as children of God. As believers, if we tell the enemy to give something up, he has to listen. We are not here to have a discussion, hope for the best or barter our way out of bondage: we speak, he listens. Unless, of course, we don't speak. In which case, I assure you that he will do the talking. He will explain that the situation is impossible, that he has the upper hand, that we don't know what we are talking about and that we will fail at whatever we attempt to do, that God has left us and that all our fears are actually true.

Quite simply: when we remain silent, the enemy takes charge.

It is our decision who will fill the airwaves of our mind, heart and soul, and if we don't want Satan there, he has to vacate the premises. To believe anything else is to elevate a lie above the truth. Because my Bible says that we can submit to God, resist the devil, and he *has* to flee.[4] There is no caveat for having a bad day and it is not dependent on spiritual, financial or emotional strength. He may not go willingly, or even immediately, but faith stands until victory is secured.

Therefore, when Jehovah Jireh[5] told Moses to demand the enemy pay him back for all the years of slavery, there was no argument and the treasures were tossed over. (Note that *God* told

Moses to ask for it: there is a time to ask and a time to wait – *wisdom discerns the time*.)

Once Moses knew the will of God, there was no hesitation (or poverty mentality) that made him doubt his ability to help others transition from slavery to prosperity. This is a beautiful picture of what Jesus did for us on the cross of Calvary. We were enslaved in our sins, unable to escape the tyranny of the enemy, but when we accepted what Jesus did on the cross for us, all the riches of heaven immediately became ours and we left our sinful life as prosperous children of the living God – no longer slaves, but now of royal inheritance.

Moses learned that the risk is worth taking, but he's about to see that leaving hiddenness may reveal challenging questions.

For Reflection

- Describe a time when you have had to stay in a place you didn't want to stay, and how you saw the Lord bring good out of a tough situation.

- What does the favour of God look like in your life?

- Is it easy for you to receive God's blessings? If not, why do you think that is, and are there choices you can make to change that?

- We must take risk in relationship. What risks do you feel God is asking you to take in your relationship with him? What is your answer?

Part Four

Trusting

12

In Battle

Because of the LORD's great love we are not con-
sumed, for his compassions never fail. They are
new every morning; great is your faithfulness.
Lam. 3:22–23

Imagine this scene: you are standing in the middle of a combat zone, war raging around you, injured soldiers screaming in pain and begging for help, shellfire exploding to your right and to your left, the stench of death overwhelming every one of your senses. The fight has grown fierce and at that moment your army is losing the war, defeat threatening to wipe out the rest of your troops. You are the general in charge, and as you fix your attention on the devastation you suddenly realize that all the soldiers are looking to you for direction. Feeling helpless (and scared) you hear yourself yelling: 'What are you looking at *me* for? You guys are the ones losing this battle! If you were better at fighting, we wouldn't be in this mess. You deserve what you're getting here!'

No good general in the middle of a battle would berate an army in that manner; they would take leadership, form a strategy and lead them towards victory. Winston Churchill famously said: 'Fear is a reaction. Courage is a decision.'[1]

Blame is a victim's response, often grown from seeds of insecurity and fear. We choose to put the focus anywhere other than our personal responsibility because, if it is someone else's fault, then the consequences are out of our control. This is used with God all the time. (I raise my hands as 'guilty as charged' along with everyone else!)

'God, why did you, didn't you, couldn't you, wouldn't you . . .' fill the mouth of every Christian at one time or another. I remember sobbing on the floor – gut-wrenching sobs of pain – grieving for the children I would never have and yelling to the Lord: 'I have given everything up for you . . . could you not give me the one thing that I have desired in life?'

The pain was overwhelming and the judgment against God was searing hot with emotion and accusation. When we find ourselves in positions we have not asked for, it is our natural instinct to project our pain onto someone else – often one we trust the most and love the deepest.

Moses had been living a quiet life, enjoying his wife and children, shepherding his flock in Midian far from the past, forging a new hope for his future. He was not looking to be the saviour of a nation, he was not seeking fame and glory, and he was certainly not expecting to write the first five books of the Old Testament or carry the Ten Commandments in his own hands (twice). As we saw earlier, Moses had absolutely no idea what was in store for his future; he had carved out a new normal, relaxing into routine and comfort once again.

Our quiet seasons are often preparation for our greatest battles. I don't believe Moses' greatest fight was facing Pharaoh, enduring the Israelites or eyeballing the Red Sea. I think it was internal – it was the small voice inside his head that told him that he

> Our quiet seasons are often preparation for our greatest battles.

had no voice, that he was a poor leader and that there were others far more qualified for this job. His lack of confidence is glaringly obvious within the first four chapters of Exodus. As we've read, Moses complains five times about his lack of lucid speech and leadership ability – clearly refusing to believe he was the man for the job. Reading those chapters, it gets repetitive to the point of nausea and this is the reason Aaron, Moses' Hebrew brother, was summoned to speak in his place. I don't believe this was God's original plan, but in his grace he allowed Moses to have help in fulfilling his calling.

Even with Aaron at his side, the choice to face, and overcome, his greatest fears was still a solitary fight. If he wanted to win, Moses must answer two all-impor-

> Is God good and can God be trusted?

tant questions in times of pain: is God good and can God be trusted?

Is God Good?

When something bad happens in your life, is your immediate response to say 'God, why?' Do you get defensive with the Lord, assuming the victim role, angry that a God of love would allow something so cruel?

As previously mentioned, dialoguing with God is good, and sharing how we truly feel is necessary. He is not afraid of our anger, nor is he manipulated by our tears. God has a profound love for his children and deeply grieves alongside us as we process what we cannot control. But if we allow ourselves to repeatedly doubt his goodness, demanding an explanation for the inexplicable, then we *will* impede our spiritual maturity.

Why do we assume that this world should be trial free? Trials and challenges can be used by God to strengthen our faith to the point where we can believe for more than is naturally possible. This will only happen if we allow it to be so; if we get intimidated and distracted by the lie that God is punishing us or trying to teach us a lesson, then it will be increasingly difficult to draw near to one we believe is deliberately hurting us. That is akin to child abuse and clearly does not resemble a loving parent. With that being said, God can use the situation to teach, mould, shape and prepare us for the opportunity he has in our future to bring glory to him and purpose to us.

As we have seen earlier in the book, it is impossible to develop intimacy with one we do not trust, and we will not trust one we believe gains pleasure from our pain. Therefore, more often than not the issue is goodness – not trust. We work diligently at trying to trust God, because the Bible says we should trust him (Prov. 3:5–6), but we miss out on the key factor to build that trust – believing in his inerrant goodness. We must believe that he desires good things for our lives, that he is acting *at all times* for our goodness and that he will work all things together for our good, as we trust in him.

Trust and goodness go hand in hand; if you are struggling to trust him, evaluate whether or not you truly believe he is good. If you don't, ask Holy Spirit to give you revelation on the nature of God (love, goodness, kindness, purity, etc.) so that you can develop trust in the actions of God, because it is impossible for him to act separately from his nature. Therefore, if his nature is good then his actions must, at their core, also be good. I believe Moses trusted the nature of God; therefore he could trust the ways of God while further deepening his walk with God.

Note the progression: it begins with knowing his nature, then trusting his ways, which leads to increasing in intimacy.

Grow beyond Fear

In the last chapter we saw Moses confronting Pharaoh in Egypt, but I want us to revisit Midian for a moment. After his conversation with God at the bush, Moses returned to Jethro, his father-in-law, and sought permission to take his wife and children with him back to Egypt. Not telling Jethro the full story, he received permission and soon found himself returning to a place he had never expected to see again. God had already assured him that those seeking his life were no longer alive, but I can imagine the uncertainty and insecurity must have increased with every passing mile.

I find it interesting that *after* Moses packed up everything and left, God informs him that Pharaoh will refuse to let the Israelites leave (Exod. 4:21–23) and that he would, in fact, harden Pharaoh's heart. In some commentaries there has been confusion as to what exactly this means and whether or not God is really to blame for the death of the Egyptians – if he did, in fact, harden the heart of the leader. My opinion is that God desires all to seek repentance and be in relationship with him, but he also knows what is in a person's heart. It was only after Pharaoh hardened his own heart against God repeatedly that we finally read in Exodus 9:12 that God hardened his heart; in other words, God withheld mercy and allowed the true nature and will of Pharaoh to be done in his life and, consequently, in the lives of the people he was leading.

Have you ever stepped out in obedience, sure that the decision you were making was the leading of the Lord, only to have it go wrong? Perhaps it was a relationship that didn't progress as you thought it would or an investment that fell apart. I remember many years ago, before moving to the UK, that I felt the Lord show me a relationship that would become very significant in my life. It took me by surprise, but there were so many confirmations that I could not ignore it. I was certain this was of the Lord . . . but it was not.

Obviously, whenever other people are involved, even the most accurate prophetic words may not come to pass, but regardless of the reason, for a long time this outcome left me with confusion and a fear of trusting my ability to hear God's voice. If I had got *that* wrong, how would I ever trust my discernment again? Looking back, it's clear that I had a prophetic call on my life and the enemy was working extremely hard to dislodge a growing gift. Sadly it took me well over twenty years before I realized that, and many opportunities to step out and grow in the gift were missed as a result.

On the other hand, perhaps you have wilfully disobeyed the Lord and are reaping the consequences of that decision, and now are fearful of letting him down again. Yes, we reap what we sow, but we also serve a God who is kind, forgiving and loving, and who is ready to receive the prodigal home. Moses left Egypt in disobedience, his entire future in disarray, yet now God was allowing him to return in humility – asking Moses to trust him.

If we want to move out of hiddenness we must grow beyond fearfulness.

This is the third key towards leaving hiddenness and walking in holiness: refuse to let fear control your decisions any longer.

> If we want to move out of hiddenness we must grow beyond fearfulness.

Whether it is fear of God's anger or fear of getting it wrong, fear will never grow intimacy. I once heard a preacher say: 'Nobody is afraid of flying; they are afraid of dying!' That is true; it is the fear of death which is the root of all fear – death of a relationship, dream, opportunity, or even a life. Moses was fearing death as he returned to the place where he had delivered death; there must have been some trepidation over this irony. He learned to overcome that fear over time, and though he had ample opportunity to blame the people of Israel for their lack of faith, critical spirit and full-on rebellion, he only chose blame once (yet that one time changed the trajectory of his future).[2]

As we will see, the real issue is not blame; it is trust.

Vulnerable

There is a video making the rounds right now on social media where a 'trust exercise' is being done at an office staff training session. The exercise has one person stand on a chair, close his eyes, and when the leader gives the go ahead . . . he falls. Meanwhile, before he falls, the rest of the staff gather in two lines facing one another, with their arms outstretched, ready to catch the one falling. Because the person's eyes are closed, he must trust that he will not crash to the ground when he allows himself to fall. In this video everyone is set, the group is standing behind the man ready to catch him, and once the leader says 'Go' the man falls . . . forward! The video cuts out just as he is crashing face first onto the ground, with a group of team members behind him with hands – and mouths – wide open.

Misplaced trust can be painful.

Trust seems easy to ask from others, but painful to give ourselves. Trust begets trust and we cannot have trust without vulnerability; the two go hand in hand. In order to grow in trust, we must move in risk. Moses had no idea what would happen to him when he approached Pharaoh. He must have had all sorts of feelings and emotions swirling around as he and his family approached the land, and the home, where he had spent his growing-up years. Would God protect him or was he walk-ing towards his death?

Making ourselves vulnerable to another human being is one thing; being vulnerable with God is quite another. Humans we can see, respond to and interact with, but how do you respond to one you cannot see or hear (at least in the natural realm)? If we have a strong sense of God as a God of love then that makes it easier, but if there is any misunderstanding of the nature or character of God, then we will struggle to open ourselves up to a level required for major steps of faith and depths of intimacy. If I think God will hold anything I say or do against me, I'm going to struggle to draw near to him when I am hurting, confused or in sin – the very times I *need* to be drawing near to him.

I often tell people to invite God into their sin. When they are doing, saying, thinking something they are ashamed of or that they know is wrong (whether it be emotional, sexual, men-tal or physical), that is the time to let the Lord take a seat at the table, so to speak. First, so they will know they are accepted no matter what they do; second, to invite Holy Spirit into a place where he can give direction and guidance; and third, to let the enemy know he cannot hold this over their head as a secret – God already knows about it. (I realize he does anyway, but I think intentionally inviting him in is like removing the fuse to the dynamite of lie held in the hand of the enemy.)

> God is never the enemy: the enemy is the enemy.

Blame can be deadly, but blaming God is pointless. God is never the enemy: the enemy is the enemy. We all face battles in life; some arrive as medical impossibilities and others show up through forever relationships . . . that didn't last forever. The easiest thing to do at those times is to hide in our anger and fear, allowing the enemy to keep us from the very one who can heal the hurt and bring something good out of something evil.

Moses had to revisit his place of pain, and disobedience, in order for this to happen. He had to see the faithfulness of God despite his own unfaithfulness. Through each of the plagues released on the Egyptians, Moses grew in confidence and trust – realizing that faithfulness follows into our wilderness and that battles not only test us but also ultimately grow us.

For Reflection

- Do you believe that God is good and that God can be trusted? If not, spend some time meditating or journaling on why this is and consider whether you would like this to change or not.

- 'If we want to move out of hiddenness we must grow beyond fearfulness.' What would this look like for you?

- Does it scare you to become vulnerable with God? Why or why not?

- How do you feel at the thought of inviting God into your sin, that is, allowing him to be part of your journey of freedom, without shame?

13

No Way Out

The LORD will fight for you; you need only to be still.

                                                        Exod. 14:14

Recently I was in America for Thanksgiving and my sister and I were enjoying a meal out with our parents. It had been many years since only the four of us had been out to dinner (without her husband or my brother and his family) and we quickly began reminiscing. My sister has a memory like a vault (whereas mine is more like that of a goldfish) so we relied on Tammi to walk us down memory lane. It wasn't long before we found ourselves laughing our way through the meal. Suddenly Tammi looked at me and said, 'Remember when we got locked in the hallway closet for a few hours?'

Ummm . . . no.

But the more she talked, the clearer the memory became, and suddenly I was about 4 years old again stuck in a dark closet, certain I would never escape. I debated whether or not to include this story because it sounds like my mom and dad should be taken in for child neglect, but please believe me when I say they were brilliant parents – this was simply not one of their greatest moments.

We had bought a new swing set and my parents were out-side needing a degree in engineering so that they could as-semble the blessed thing. At the time, they thought their two little girls (my sister being one year older than me) would be fine playing inside the house by themselves, while they wrestled with the disassembled chaos outside. None of us could remember how long they were gone, but it vacillated between ten minutes and three hours – depending on who you asked.

My sister had the marvellous idea that we should hide from Mom and Dad so that when they came inside they would have an enforced game of hide-and-seek to play. We chose to lie low in the upstairs closet, giggling as we squished ourselves into the tiny space, imagining the surprise on our parents' faces when they finally found us. As we knelt down, Tammi reached her little hand up between the shelves and the door knob and slowly closed the door, removing her hand quickly to avoid it getting squashed. It never occurred to our young minds that as a result of the shelf above our heads, it was now impossible to reopen the door from the inside.

We were stuck.

The first few minutes of giggling were great fun, but then I got scared. Once I got an idea in my little 'red-in-the-head' (my dad's nickname for me as I had bright-red hair) imagina-tion, it was impossible to remove it. Suddenly I envisaged us never being found, causing my heart rate to increase, my tem-perature to rise and my insides to begin rumbling. I needed out and I needed out *now*! My sister tried reaching the doorknob, and upon realizing she couldn't, my panic went into overdrive. Ever the pragmatic and logical one, she tried to calm me down, which only increased my panic to the point of . . . throwing up all over her shoes.

Feeling trapped – whether physically, emotionally, mentally or spiritually – can quickly evoke irrational feelings. So now we were two little girls stuck in a small closet, with no parents in the house, covered in smelly vomit. It really is quite extraordinary that I didn't remember this story until my sister began re-telling it that November evening, over forty years later. As I said, my parents were great parents, so although it seemed like it was a few hours before they found us, realistically it was more like fifteen minutes. Instead of finding two giggling girls laughing at their prank, my mother found two (well, at least one) crying young girl, covered in vomit, certain she was going to die next to her sister and a broomstick.

Being stuck is never enjoyable.

Whether it is being stuck in traffic, a relationship, a job or the broom closet, if we aren't careful, immobilization will pave the way for destabilization. Once Pharaoh finally gave the go-ahead for the Israelites to leave, Moses found himself stuck at an impasse called the Red Sea. He had led several thousand people into this dead end, and they wanted answers.

Where Do You Go?

I'll say it again: we must never limit an unlimited God.

> We must never limit an unlimited God.

When Moses faced this large, liquid impasse, he had not yet read the book of Exodus. He was living this out in real time, without the benefit of knowing that God would convert the Red Sea into a red carpet of escape. Moses had grown up in the Egyptian household and he knew the bloodthirsty tactics of the Egyptian army; after losing his firstborn son, Pharaoh was not in the mood to negotiate. To make matters worse, Moses' life was not only in danger from the Egyptians but also from his own people – they were out for his blood.

Exodus 14:11–12 says:

> They said to Moses, 'Was it because there were no graves in Egypt that you brought us to the desert to die? What have you done to us by bringing us out of Egypt? Didn't we say to you in Egypt, "Leave us alone; let us serve the Egyptians"? It would have been better for us to serve the Egyptians than to die in the desert!'

Having spent four hundred years in slavery and a relatively short time in freedom, it is still surprising that the first sign of difficulty made them long for bondage over believing. True, the challenge was not a small-town traffic jam, but still . . . to wish for a painful past over a confusing present is to be completely void of faith.

We need to be a church that knows how to fight and to fight well. Not from a stance of anger, rudeness and trolling on social media, but from a place of *faith*.

Faith sees what others cannot see and it believes what others refuse to believe, experiencing what others long to experience. Moses never physically saw God in the burning bush, but he believed it was God. It is important to remember: sight did not cause him to leave the familiar – faith did.

Andrew Murray says: 'Recognize Him in everything that happens. Seek to walk in the light of His countenance. Seeing the Invisible will make it easy to forsake the world and to do the will of God.'[1]

Faith stands. It does not back down, step down or sit down in the face of opposition and criticism. It stays silent, unless directed to speak, and it stays humble, even when wrongly accused. We see this beautifully in Jesus when he stood before his accusers, yet refused to speak or acknowledge their misjudgment of his character. If we falter at every little criticism, we will never mature beyond our need for outward acceptance into a strong, inner confidence born out of a secure identity in Christ.

> If we falter at every little criticism, we will never mature beyond our need for outward acceptance into a strong, inner confidence born out of a secure identity in Christ.

As a shepherd, Moses had spent years in the desert separated from his family and alone with God. He had learned that God was trustworthy, even when he himself was unfaithful. So, with the faithless cries of those behind him, he carefully measured how he was going to respond to the current crisis. We have already seen that Moses was not keen to speak, and in this case that played in his favour.

Speak What You See

I cannot emphasize enough the importance of watching our words when trouble comes. What we speak influences our perception, and our perception dictates how we respond. If I speak negativity and fear, then I increase my chances of seeing impossibility and death, because that is the filter through which I view my circumstances. We cannot speak fear and act in faith; the two are as incompatible with one another as water and oil. If we want to walk in spiritual maturity and holiness, it is better to remain silent than speak unbelief. Doubt causes instability, and oscillation causes confusion, and then confusion clouds our ability to think clearly. At least by saying nothing we give ourselves the opportunity to strengthen our faith before we say anything foolish!

I realize how difficult this is to do, but I challenge you to try it for a season (not only a day) and then watch and see what happens. Very likely, the minute you start to change your negative and fear-filled words to something positive and faith-filled, you will find yourselves thinking things like *This is crazy*, *It's just words*, and so on. I believe the battle itself is a clear indicator that it is worth doing. Positive thinking started in the Bible, not with the New Age movement – but the enemy challenges truth, because he wants us to believe a lie. If he is fighting against us taking authority over our minds, then that is a sure sign there is victory to be had by taking captive every thought and making it obedient to Christ.

Romans 12:2 says: 'Do not conform to the pattern of this world, but be transformed by the renewing of your mind. Then you will be able to test and approve what God's will is – his good, pleasing and perfect will.'

As we are intentional about what we say, our thinking is transformed. Once our thoughts and words are in agreement with a new way of thinking and speaking, then our actions will follow suit. We cannot behave in a way we do not believe – at least not in the long term. So the place to begin is with our thoughts and words. Intentionally taking captive our thoughts to his will, and walking in obedience to his leading, is what opens the door to behavioural change and, eventually, begins building a road back to the type of fellowship that originated in the Garden of Eden.

This Is How We Fight

There is a popular song out now called 'Surrounded (Fight My Battles)' that talks about how to fight the battles we are facing.

One phrase shares the truth that although our circumstances, or the enemy, surround us, there is something greater still that surrounds both us and the enemy – God's presence and power. I love that. Regardless of how many enemies are surrounding us, how many weapons are being formed against us, or how many impossibilities stare us down . . . in that very place we are surrounded by the love and protection of our Saviour.[2]

Have you ever tried carrying several packages or bags from the car into the house at one time, finding yourself dropping things because you picked up more than was wise? Or perhaps you were holding your toddler in your arms while trying to cook dinner at the same time, without much success. In the same way, we cannot hold peace and anxiety simultaneously in our hearts – one or the other must go. If we allow anxiety and worry any space in our minds or hearts, it will grow to the point of exhaustion – or at the very least it will make a home for peace untenable.

But as we intentionally acknowledge the truth of God's protection, putting pressure on that promise, we will see the enemy fade from our spiritual peripheral vision as the glory and goodness of Almighty God becomes more real than our fear. Moses did not turn around or in any way engage with the enemy; he stood his ground, declared his faith, listened for instructions and spoke the truth.

I love how Exodus 14:13–14 is written in the Amplified Bible (AMPC, emphasis mine):

Moses told the people, Fear not; stand still (*firm, confident, undismayed*) and see the salvation of the Lord which He will work for you today. For the Egyptians you have seen today you shall never see again. The Lord will fight for you, and you shall hold your peace and remain at rest.

That is a clear picture of how we are meant to fight battles: firm, confident, undismayed. Perhaps you need to write this down, put it on your mirror and make this one of your morning declarations: 'I will not move in fear, I stand strong in faith and I refuse to be swayed by what I see!'

> I will not move in fear, I stand strong in faith and I refuse to be swayed by what I see!

Say it out loud once again: 'I will not move in fear, I stand strong in faith and I refuse to be swayed by what I see!'

It feels pretty good, doesn't it? The more we say the truth, the brighter our faith shines through. We build that faith muscle in the same way we develop biceps when we use the resistance of weight to shape and form them into the muscles they were created to be. Faith is what overcomes the world and is what moves mountains, or – as we have seen for Moses – moves whatever is blocking our way to the Promised Land.

Our responsibility is to hold our peace, stand strong and remain at rest, letting the Lord fight on our behalf.

Fighting for the Future

Moses had the assurance of God that he would be with him and that he would give him Aaron as a mouthpiece to assist in seeing his will be done. Standing at the Red Sea, Moses needed to believe the word of God more than he believed the sound of the enemy. He knew the enemy was closing in and he knew that death was their only aim. When we stare death in the face it is nearly impossible to stay in peace; only by the grace of God can we stand our ground and refuse to let the grip of fear win. The Bible says the following:

Say to those with fearful hearts, 'Be strong, do not fear; your God will come, he will come with vengeance; with divine retribution he will come to save you.'

Isa. 35:4

Have I not commanded you? Be strong and courageous. Do not be afraid; do not be discouraged, for the LORD your God will be with you wherever you go.

Josh. 1:9

I sought the LORD, and he answered me; he delivered me from all my fears.

Ps. 34:4

The LORD is my light and my salvation – whom shall I fear? The LORD is the stronghold of my life – of whom shall I be afraid?'

Ps. 27:1

To live in victory, we must choose to believe that fear (or any scheme of the enemy) is not stronger than God's word. If we believe that God and his word have more power than the enemy and fear itself, we can begin to take authority over fear in our lives. I am not saying it is easy, nor am I saying we simply repeat a scripture once and then the enemy flees in terror. I wish that were the case!

But believing that a particular circumstance, person, report or challenge holds greater power than God will automatically enthrone that lie over God's truth. The truth is: cancer is not greater than God; poverty is not greater than God; rebellion is not greater than God. God will always have the final word – even death must bow its knee to eternal life!

However, if we agree with the lies of the enemy and/or choose to distance ourselves from God through our anger, then we open the door to all sorts of evil and destruction. Because one thing that *is* greater than God, if we allow it to be, is our self-will. God gave us free will and, by doing so, he gave us the ability to enthrone something or someone above himself. Once we make that choice, legally he cannot force us to change. But once we decide that God's word, nature and character will have the final authority in our life, and we put them in their rightful place as Lord, then the enemy must bow to God's sovereignty. In that place is where I choose to put my trust.

This choice to stand and believe God over his circumstances was the fourth important decision Moses made that helped lead him out of hiddenness and towards a life displaying greater holiness.

> This choice to stand and believe God over his circumstances was the fourth important decision Moses made which helped lead him out of hiddenness and towards a life displaying greater holiness.

Standing in faith takes repetition, perseverance, a refusal to quit and a belief that is stronger than feelings. If Moses had gone by what he felt (fear) or what he saw (a wall of water in front and the enemy pursuing him behind), he and the Israelites would have all died, or at the very least been enslaved again. What would have happened to Joshua and Caleb? Would the people have eventually escaped and would Joshua still have taken them into the Promised Land?

We don't need to speculate because Moses had the courage to stand his ground and listen for his next instruction – a decision that would soon be repeated as Moses faced his next big test: the wilderness.

For Reflection

- Have you ever felt as if you were at a Red Sea in life? What did you do? How did it end?

- What would it look like if you stopped limiting God? What would you believe for?

- Would you be willing to take a challenge that for thirty days (or one day!) you wouldn't speak anything negative? It's a wonderful group activity to do, so you can encourage one another in the challenging moments!

- Where do you right now need to believe God's word over what you see in the natural realm? Take time to declare his goodness, grace and sovereignty in your life and circumstances.

14

Through the Wilderness

Even though I walk through the darkest valley,
I will fear no evil, for you are with me; your rod
and your staff, they comfort me.

Ps. 23:4

Can you thank God in advance for what will astound you upon reflection?

His love is one constant that never fails to astound me. I have seen him work many miracles in my life, yet the fact that he sent his only Son to die on a cross for my sins continues to take my breath away in wonder. Perhaps you are astounded by his faithfulness, kindness, love, tenderness, forgiveness or mercy. Have you thanked him today for that?

He doesn't need our gratitude, but he enjoys it. I don't think it's because he is a selfish God who takes pride in being praised; instead, he enjoys connecting with us on a level far deeper than 'Why, God, why?' and 'When, God, when?' As we praise him for his nature, we are loving him for who he is, not for what he does.

Taking a few minutes to be grateful is a worthwhile daily exercise.

Moses had just passed the 'impossibility test', watching as the Red Sea miraculously bowed to the freedom of several thousand slaves. Once the Israelites had safely passed, the sea resumed its given domain, swallowing up an army of Egyptians in the process. There was hardly time for celebration before Moses' next test appeared – a test that would weigh on him for the next forty years:

> Then Moses led Israel from the Red Sea and they went into the Desert of Shur. For three days they travelled in the desert without finding water. When they came to Marah, they could not drink its water because it was bitter. (That is why the place is called Marah.) So the people grumbled against Moses, saying, 'What are we to drink?'[1]

Lack would soon become daily life, and dependence on God a necessity. In other words, water supply wasn't the real test – the wilderness was. This was the beginning of the Israelites living astounded, or at least being presented with the opportunity to live astounded:

> Then Moses cried out to the LORD, and the LORD showed him a piece of wood. He threw it into the water, and the water became fit to drink.
> There the LORD issued a ruling and instruction for them and put them to the test. He said, 'If you listen carefully to the LORD your God and do what is right in his eyes, if you pay attention to his commands and keep all his decrees, I will not bring on you any of the diseases I brought on the Egyptians, for I am the LORD, who heals you.'

Then they came to Elim, where there were twelve springs and seventy palm trees, and they camped there near the water.[2]

Moses had seen the water part and now he sees the water purified; even if the people cannot acknowledge God's help, Moses' trust in the Lord must be growing with each miracle. But the miracles came with a condition: if they listen and pay attention to the Lord's commandments then they will remain healed and whole. In other words, blessing follows obedience.

This is a truth seen throughout the Bible. We do not work for blessings, but we do reap what we sow, and if we sow to the spirit we will reap from the spirit eternal life – a life that is described as *shalom* (wholeness, peace and prosperity). Being thankful in a wilderness season is one of the most challenging tests we must face. It contends with our flesh, pride, emotions and thoughts. Habitual thankfulness contests the cultural norm and seems counter-intuitive to what we feel: I'm lying if I say that I'm thankful for how I'm feeling . . . because I am not!

It takes seeing the end from the beginning and discerning the miracle out of the moment. I am not thanking him for the crisis, pain or battle, but I am thanking him for the victory on the other side of the battle. I am thanking him that he is greater than any battle I face and that there is absolutely nothing the enemy can do that has more power than the God I am in covenant with at this moment.

In other words, I am thanking him now for the miracle I expect to see in the future.

This choice to be intentionally thankful is our next key in transitioning from hiddenness to holiness because a heart of gratitude is motivated by love, expressing the very nature of God himself.

This choice to be intentionally thankful is our next key in transitioning from hiddenness to holiness because a heart of gratitude is motivated by love, expressing the very nature of God himself.

As we emulate his nature, submitting our flesh to the spirit, holiness will become a natural outworking of a supernatural choice.

Ventilator Faith

I know what you are thinking: *But what if I thank him for the miracle and then I don't receive it?*

For most of my life I thought the same way and would have responded with that same thought. I would try to think positive, but I felt like a fraud repeating words I wasn't convinced were coming to pass in my life. It would be good to remind ourselves of the definition of a fraud. My personal definition is someone using information without permission for unjust gain. If we take that definition and apply it to a born-again believer declaring words given to us by God himself, it doesn't apply.

First of all, we are speaking words he has *asked* us to speak (Phil. 4:8; Eph. 4:29) and we are speaking words that will not only build us up, but also build up those around us. We become fraudulent when we stop trusting that the words will come to pass or if we use Scripture attempting to manipulate others (or God) into doing something for our benefit.

Scripture is not meant to be a quick fix, nor can we pick and choose a verse to declare, expecting the Lord to suddenly bow to our demands. 'In Jesus' name' isn't a phrase that we casually tag onto the end of whatever we want, assuming God will jump to attention because we used the 'magic words'. This isn't about taking words out of context to suit our situation; it is necessary to study the scriptures that we are speaking, to avoid the trap of extremism and false teaching.

With that being said, there are numerous scriptures that speak about not doubting and believing that what you pray will come to pass. A few of my favourites are Mark 11:22–24;

Matthew 21:22; Isaiah 55:11; and Hebrews 11:3. None of the above scriptures have results coming from what is seen, but all see impossibilities happening because of faith and the unseen.

Please trust me – I understand the challenge! Most of my Christian life was spent trying to figure out how to marry these verses with unanswered prayers and hesitant hopes, lived out through weakened faith. Often I would say to the Lord, 'I feel like my faith is on a ventilator.' I would go to a great Sunday meeting and my faith would get inflated again so I felt I could breathe spiritually, but after a few days of speaking doubt and negativity I would feel weak, and once again everything looked impossible. I was finding that I couldn't speak faith out of weakened spiritual lungs.

Then one day I was challenged by a friend to believe Scripture over circumstances. That's easy to say when there's a logical way to solve an issue, but when you are standing in front of a complete impossibility, needing a miracle to survive, you will soon discover whether or not you really believe what you say you believe. I was in the greatest wilderness season of my life when I began diligently studying, and applying, these principles I am sharing.

> Deciding that the Bible would be the final authority in my life . . . was one of the best decisions of my life.

Deciding that the Bible would be the final authority in my life, and that I would never put what I saw in the natural realm above what I believed in the spiritual, was one of the best decisions of my life. I am not saying it was easy – it was not, and is still not!

In, But Not Of . . .

Recently I have spoken with several women who are struggling with the fact that they are over 35 and single. I often have that conversation with women who are believing for a husband and children yet for whatever reason everyone in their world seems to be getting married except them. As I mentioned earlier, I understand singleness! I have prayed, cried, fasted, agonized and bargained with God, but all to no avail. I was even close to adoption – very close – at one point in my life when the rug was pulled out from under me and the whole process came to a screeching halt. I don't have vocabulary to describe the depth of pain I felt at that disappointment.

I have a friend right now whose young daughter is battling cancer, another who lost both parents this past year, another who is unsure how she and her husband will feed their family because finances are so tight, another whose marriage is hanging on by a thread, another who has just lost her job, another . . . and another . . . and another. Pain and disappointment are rife and are no respecter of persons – we will all face pain and disappointment in this world, because we are in this world. But we are not *of* this world, and those two letters ('of' instead of 'in') make a tremendous difference to our response.

It only took the Israelites *three days* to go from elation and exultation to exasperation and excommunication – they turned on Moses, even after he had saved them through the Red Sea. People are fickle and leadership is lonely. Pain and disappointment are powerful and they quickly bring to the forefront what is happening behind the scenes. What we say in these seasons will determine how much God can trust us.

Out of the overflow of the heart, the mouth truly does speak (Matt. 12:34); so listen to what you say, in order to gauge whether you have a heart of worship or an attitude of negativity.

Maturity speaks truth, not facts. If we want to further God's kingdom and fulfil our life assignment 'down to the last detail',[3] then we must carry a heart of thanksgiving, in spite of what we see.

The thing about the wilderness is that in that place you have plenty of time to think, and that is even more reason to be intentional in your choices of what you will allow in and what you will keep out.

Empty Spaces

Have you ever been in a conversation with someone who was not comfortable with silence? Hardly two seconds passes between you before they are talking about something, anything, in order to fill the void of noise. Those people always made me uncomfortable, until I noticed myself doing the same thing. I am certainly not like that in all relationships, but there are specific times where I find myself speaking before thinking and nervously filling space that perhaps might be better left unfilled. It happens when I am uneasy or when I think the other person expects me to have an answer; in other words, when there is pressure to perform.

Do we ever do that with God, I wonder? When he is silent, and seems distant, do we feel a pressure to act right/be right/do right in order to win the pleasure of his acceptance, and sense of presence, again? Is that perhaps our way of 'filling the space' and covering the distance that is too uncomfortable to endure? Wilderness is filled with space; that is part of its definition and identity. As wonderful as it may sound, living in a place without boundaries creates unease, because we were not created for freedom without borders. Healthy boundaries are there to keep us safe, not hold us back.

> Healthy boundaries are there to keep us safe, not hold us back.

Years ago a study was done on the effect of the fence in a school playground.

The researchers discovered that when there was no fence, the children would tend to play in the centre of the playground, not venturing out very far. But once there was a fence, the children would play to the very edge of the boundary, using all the space available to them. The article summarized this finding by saying: 'Fences brought freedom. It was the absence of fences that created fear and apprehension.'[4]

In the wilderness of life, God's word is a fence. When we grow in maturity with the Lord, and learn the dangers of living outside his word and obedience, then we are ready to be given a choice. This is imperative for our growth because to know that freedom exists, and yet not have the choice to enjoy it, is not a boundary, but a prison. Choice allows us to explore the boundaries within our wilderness. As we obey, we experience more and more blessings, growing our maturity and preparing us for the blessing that lies on the other side of our wilderness season.

As Moses led the people into the wilderness and they experienced freedom for the first time in hundreds of years, their first response was to grumble and to complain. They were complaining because the answer looked different from what they had expected. They wanted the fullness of freedom without the bother of challenge. As we all do.

Soon the Lord gave them a test: he asked Moses to send spies into the Promised Land he was giving to them. This was the most obvious open-book test ever created, as God had already explained the land was theirs – all they needed to do was come back with a good report. Sadly, that was too much to ask. They continued complaining and rebelling to the point where, when they were presented with the Promised Land, and everything they had been dreaming of for years . . . they didn't want it.

The wilderness had become so entrenched in them that there was no longer any good soil in which the seed of promise could grow. I go into much more detail on this subject in my book *The Power of a Promise*,[5] so if you find yourself facing disappointments with God that you are struggling to move beyond, or have promises from heaven you have been waiting on for years, I would strongly recommend that you get a copy of that book.

If we refuse to remove the wilderness from our vision, words and thinking, then there is literally no hope for us to receive the holy, abundant life that God promised. That is harsh, but it is the truth.

The wilderness seasons are challenging, beautiful, empowering and defining . . . but only if we press in to the goodness of God and allow them to be. In the wilderness, through forty years of lack, Moses (and the Israelites) experienced Jehovah Jireh, the God Who Provides. He started by purifying their water and continued by feeding them manna every day for the rest of their lives. He did not fail them, even one time. Not a single day of manna was missed (except for the Sabbath, which was provided for by doubling the amount falling the day before), every week, fifty-two weeks a year, for forty years. If my calculations are right, that is approximately 12,480 times that God provided enough food to adequately feed several million people . . . in a *desert*.

And I wonder if he can find me a husband.

God literally has a million ways to answer every prayer request. We must get a revelation that miracles are *not* difficult for God!

A miracle to God is like breathing to us. We breathe, because that is what we were created to do. He provides, because that is what he was created to do.

> A miracle to God is like breathing to us. We breathe, because that is what we were created to do. He provides, because that is what he was created to do.

Moses saw this day in and day out, miracle after miracle after miracle, provision after provision after provision, blessing after blessing after blessing . . . and each encounter increased his understanding of the nature and character of God: faithful, good, true and loving.

Not a God to be feared in hiddenness but, as we can now begin to discover, a God to be known in holiness.

For Reflection

- Do you find it easy to thank God for things before you have received them? Why or why not?

- Are there areas in your life where you feel you have 'ventilator faith'?

- Can you easily rest in silence with the Lord? If not, try setting an alarm for ten minutes and just be quiet; intentionally bring your thoughts back to him when they wander. What did you learn from that? Did he say anything to you? Were you able to rest?

15

On the Mountain

You shall have no other gods before me.

Exod. 20:3

As a teenager I dated a young man who was trouble, though I didn't realize it at the time because I was simply pleased that someone liked me. To give you an idea of his character: he would tell me I was beautiful one minute and then a few minutes later he would ask why I was wearing that belt 'because it makes you look fat'.

Yeah, a real winner.

I'll never forget the day he asked me why I never initiated kissing him. Being deeply insecure meant there was no way I would have *ever* made the first move on a guy. I told him as much and so, with a sinister smile, he declared that he was not going to get out of the car until I kissed him. Oh, the agony, embarrassment and shame I felt at the thought of leaning towards him and initiating a kiss. At that time I had no knowledge of the abuse from my childhood, so the fear was palpable but I didn't understand why it was so deep. After five minutes of trembling and trying to get out of it, I finally worked up the courage to give him a very quick kiss, when at the last second he pulled away. I was left looking ridiculous, puckered up mid-air, while he laughed in my face. It was a horrible thing to do and I still remember the shame and embarrassment I felt.

For years I wondered if God was like Shawn[1] – would I work up the courage to get close, only to have him laugh in my face and back away because I was suddenly unacceptable to him? Of course, now I know that would *never* happen, but when you have experienced abuse, it is sometimes difficult to separate the abuser from the healer.

> When you have experienced abuse it is sometimes difficult to separate the abuser from the healer.

The bottom line was that, in order to develop closeness (and experience healing), I had to give God access to my heart . . . and to my pain.

In Exodus 19 we see God preparing Moses and the people to receive the Ten Commandments, but first this required some preparation. Initially they were up for the challenge, as we see here in Exodus 19:3–8:

> Then Moses went up to God, and the LORD called to him from the mountain and said, 'This is what you are to say to the descendants of Jacob and what you are to tell the people of Israel: "You yourselves have seen what I did to Egypt, and how I carried you on eagles' wings and brought you to myself. Now if you obey me fully and keep my covenant, then out of all nations you will be my treasured possession. Although the whole earth is mine, you will be for me a kingdom of priests and a holy nation." These are the words you are to speak to the Israelites.'
>
> So Moses went back and summoned the elders of the people and set before them all the words the LORD had commanded him to speak. The people all responded together, 'We will do everything

the LORD has said.' So Moses brought their answer back to the LORD.

Interestingly, the first response of the people was obedience. Then in verse 10 God spoke to Moses on Mount Sinai, instructing him that all the people were to wash their clothes, consecrate themselves and be ready for what he was about to do. God proceeded to say that there would be limits put around the mountain, and if they crossed this boundary, they would surely die. God was a holy God and the people, even consecrated, were not ready to stand in his presence. In Exodus 19:16–20 we can read what it was like for them to see the mountain from afar:

> On the morning of the third day there was thunder and lightning, with a thick cloud over the mountain, and a very loud trumpet blast. Everyone in the camp trembled. Then Moses led the people out of the camp to meet with God, and they stood at the foot of the mountain. Mount Sinai was covered with smoke, because the LORD descended on it in fire. The smoke billowed up from it like smoke from a furnace, and the whole mountain trembled violently. As the sound of the trumpet grew louder and louder, Moses spoke and the voice of God answered him.
>
> The LORD descended to the top of Mount Sinai and called Moses to the top of the mountain. So Moses went up . . .

Imagine this scene! Thunder, lightning, a loud trumpet blast, smoke like a furnace, violent trembling . . . I don't think the Lord would need to warn me to stay away; I would have no desire to draw near that display of power.

Remember the man who earlier hid his face when a bush burned? This makes the bush look like child's play, yet Moses was not fazed at all. Through all the challenges he had to face, Moses was learning that God's presence was a place of safety, not fear.

Yet those he was leading were still locked in a slave mentality that created a gap they chose to fill with the familiar, instead of with faith.

Step by Step

Up to now, Moses has transformed from fearful murderer to bold deliverer. We have studied how he got a vision beyond himself, took risks, faced fears, trusted God's words and acted with intention. Each step led him further and further from a life of hiddenness and more intentionally towards one of holiness.

Let's now pause for a moment to reflect on the *people's* response and see what we can learn from those who kept their distance:

> When the people saw the thunder and lightning and heard the trumpet and saw the mountain in smoke, they trembled with fear. They stayed at a distance and said to Moses, 'Speak to us yourself and we will listen. But do not let God speak to us or we will die.'
>
> Moses said to the people, 'Do not be afraid. God has come to test you, so that the fear of God will be with you to keep you from sinning.'
>
> *The people remained at a distance, while Moses approached the thick darkness where God was.*[2]

Here we have the Creator showing up in power and might, necessitating Moses to mediate a conversation.[3] The people had experienced God's love when he set them free and provided for their physical needs – let alone violently destroying the enemy in front of them – yet they were still afraid of God's presence. And for good reason.

In Exodus 19 God clearly asked the people *not* to approach, or even touch, the mountain, so of course it was right that they kept a distance. But I tend to think that if Joshua was able to go near the mountain, then anyone else who had a heart for the Lord might also have been welcomed in his presence. Which says to me they did not have a heart for their God – even after everything he had done for them to show them love, provision and protection.

Humility and obedience at the burning bush were the first steps in preparation for Moses to encounter God on the mountain. If we stand before God in humility, we can stand before people without shame. (To get a greater understanding of this, imagine

> If we stand before God in humility, we will stand before people without shame.

Moses declaring the sixth commandment to the people: you should not murder. Here was a murderer telling others not to follow in his footsteps, *yet* there was no judgment from God towards him when he spoke those words, or any hint that he was ashamed before the people.)

So let me ask: what steps do you need to take in order to experience God at a new level? Notice that in the Old Testament faith *approached* the mountain, but in the New Testament faith *moves* mountains. Perhaps it is time for your faith to go from approaching God to partnering with him? Partnership implies a deeper relationship. He is still God – I'm not disputing that – but he wants to work *with* us in fulfilling purpose in our lives.

If we, like the Israelites, live in a state of fear, needing to 'proceed with caution' from a distance, then we will never mature to intimacy. Partnership is about accomplishing something together.

This carries an attachment greater than a consumer relationship – which is about receiving only. In the Old Testament people often approached God to receive something, but in the New Testament Jesus showed us what an intimate relationship with the Father looks like – sonship (a term that includes daughters) and servanthood.

This next level of intimacy is what Moses was rapidly developing . . . and the people were repeatedly avoiding.

Virtual Reality

Remember in chapter four we talked about living in a self-obsessed, identity-deprived generation? In our world today, self has become the main character in each of our dramas and the greater good is (often) put on hold for personal gain. If it benefits me, then I am in favour of it, but if I don't receive a benefit, then I don't have time for debate. We are quick to 'like' social media posts, expressing our solidarity with those hurting through a natural disaster, but we are lax to get involved beyond a simple click and perhaps a quick prayer. Before we know it we have moved on to the next item on our social media feed and the disaster is soon forgotten. I am not being critical, as I do this too, but I am expressing how easy it is in today's society to numb reality by living virtually.

The *Message* translation puts it bluntly in Proverbs 18:1: 'Loners who care only for themselves spit on the common good.'

Social media and technology have increased the ability to be alone without feeling alone. Because we are interacting with someone virtually, it is easier to feel that we are not on our own, and yet a virtual connection is not a valid and long-lasting one. In 2017 an Action for Children report stated: 'Nearly half of 11–16 year olds find it easier to be themselves online than face-to-face and three-in-five said they would be lonely if they couldn't talk to friends via technology.'[4] Yet research also found that 'almost 10% of people aged 16 to 24 were "always or often" lonely – the highest proportion of any age group. This was more than three times higher than people aged 65 and over.'[5]

So, now we have more connection, yet less real interaction. Technology has created a distance that quite frankly cannot (and should not) meet our emotional and spiritual needs.

American psychiatrist Edward Hallowell says:

Never in human history [have] our brains had to work so much information as today. We have now a generation of people who spend many hours in front of a computer monitor or a cell phone and who are so busy in processing the information received from all directions [that] they lose the ability to think and feel. Most of this information is superficial. People are sacrificing the depth and feeling and [are] cut off from other people.[6]

This has become such a growing issue that in 2018 the British prime minister, Theresa May, appointed a Ministerial Lead on Loneliness, carrying on the effort of the Loneliness Commission set up in the name of the late Jo Cox MP. A recent UK government report stated that:

Feeling lonely often is linked to early deaths – on a par with smoking or obesity. It's also linked to increased risk of coronary heart disease and stroke; depression, cognitive decline and an increased risk of Alzheimer's. It's estimated that between 5% and 18% of UK adults feel lonely often or always. And when we feel socially rejected, it triggers a response in our brain similar to one from experiencing physical pain.[7]

If our intimacy with one another is getting devalued and diminished, how much more could it happen with a God whom we cannot see and may not fully trust? Virtual relationships are based on distance – and that separation may allow us to feel safer in what we share – but they are not realistic. True relationships are built on 'doing life together', sharing with one another, facing the ups and downs, confronting difficulties and working through them, forgiving, loving, being vulnerable, and loving beyond our own selfish desires.

We cannot develop an intimate relationship with God by checking in with him on a Sunday morning for a few hours. That is better than nothing, but it resembles a virtual relationship more than a viable one.

> We cannot develop an intimate relationship with God by checking in with him on a Sunday morning for a few hours . . . That resembles a virtual relationship more than a viable one.

Idol Worship

One way or another, the relational space will be filled – on earth and in heaven. When we try to fill the spiritual void in our hearts with anything other than the Lord, the door is opened for the enemy to substitute real love with an imitation that cannot be sustained over time, and certainly will not go into eternity. If there is distance within a marriage, that area can be filled with busyness, porn, adultery, work, food, or any other substitute for the connection that we are missing. I find it fascinating that as soon as the Israelite people decided to 'remain at a distance' from the mountain, God had to confront them on idol worship.[8]

The Bible is clear: once we distance ourselves from his true love, we make room for that emptiness to be filled with something other than his presence. The Israelites were trying to fill a void of intimacy by substituting idolatry, but sadly the gap was too wide and the temptation too great. While Moses approached holiness, they courted godlessness: 'When the people saw that Moses was so long in coming down from the mountain, they gathered round Aaron and said, "Come, make us gods who will go before us. As for this fellow Moses who brought us up out of Egypt, we don't know what has happened to him."'[9]

The Bible commentator Matthew Henry says: 'Weariness in waiting betrays to many temptations.'[10]

When we grow weary in waiting for the Lord, that is the time that we are tempted to doubt, disbelieve and get into disobedience. Don't be like the Israelites! First, note their attitude towards the leader when they say 'this fellow who brought us up out of Egypt'. *This fellow?* How about: the strong leader who stood against Pharaoh of Egypt, the impossibility of the Red Sea, the criticism of millions of angry people, who approached a mountain of fire, smoke and great terror on their behalf . . . this *fellow* was a man of God who had been used to save their lives countless times!

We all see through a glass dimly and nobody has their theology absolutely perfect, but distancing ourselves from God will always have us passing out judgment from a position of ignorance. Thankfully, over the seasons, years and challenges, Moses stepped *towards* God, developing and securing that relationship above all others. He wasn't seeking to become humble or holy, yet in pursuing a God of holiness that is exactly what happened.[11]

Our toughest seasons set us up for our most intimate moments with the Lord. I don't know how to explain that, but I do know it is true. My most challenging, painful, heart-wrenching and difficult seasons of life were the times I chose to press in to the Lord, and *every* time I have found him faithful and true – a help in times of trouble and a solid rock beneath my feet.

In the challenging moments, when answers aren't available, please don't choose blame over trust. Instead, be like David who said: 'For he alone is my safe place. His wrap-around presence always protects me as my champion defender. There's no risk of failure with God! So why would I let worry paralyze me, even when troubles multiply around me?'[12]

For Reflection

- What did Moses experience because he was willing to approach God on the mountain, through the storm?

- Do you struggle with social media addiction? (Be honest!) How does this affect your relationship with God, if it does?

- How do you think loneliness has increased in your city/country? Is the Lord asking you to do anything about that?

- Ask the Lord if there are any idols in your life . . . and what would he like you to do with them.

Part Five

Deepening

16

Living Intentionally

*And Jesus increased in wisdom and in stature
and in favour with God and man.*

Luke 2:52 ESV

Favour is given, but favour can also be grown.

In the passage from Luke above, the word 'increased' is derived from the idea of 'pioneers cutting down trees in the path of an advancing army'.[1] In other words, Jesus was intentional in removing obstacles that would limit his growth, taking ownership of his calling and purpose. Being the Son of God did not mean Jesus automatically walked in favour with God. His was not a life of ease and simplicity, all his needs being met. No, he had to grow and mature at each stage of life as we all do, removing those things that would hinder his progress and maturity in the kingdom.

Recently I was taking a few days away with the Lord when, not long after I arrived, he asked me to turn off my phone and not look at social media for five hours. You would have thought he had casually asked me to cut off my right hand with a dull knife.

Five hours? Get thee behind me.

If you want to know if you are addicted to something, tell yourself you can't have it. My response – no, my *fear* – at not having access to my mobile phone for five solid hours showed me that I had a rather unhealthy attachment to this small, inanimate object. What if someone needed to get in touch with me? (Let's forget for a moment that I was on *retreat* and anyone who would normally contact me knew that I was seeking solitude.)

I confess, I wasn't nearly as worried about an emergency as I was about missing a social media alert. The first thirty minutes were torturous – embarrassingly so – but the longer I put aside what was controlling me, the easier it became to regain control.

> The longer I put aside what was controlling me, the easier it became to regain control.

Intentionality and choice have greater power than most of us like to admit. Addiction doesn't happen overnight and neither will breakthrough, but every small step moves us nearer to our destination. Once our decisions have been consistent enough to create momentum, then we will have a fighting chance against whatever has been controlling us.

As Jesus did through his choices, we also have the ability to create spiritual momentum in our lives. Terri Savelle Foy often says in her writing and podcasts that it's not *where* we start, but *whether* we start. In other words, stop procrastinating and simply do something. Don't hit snooze, put down the doughnut, turn off the phone, refuse offence, cut up the credit cards, stop hiding . . . Choose one time to respond differently in that situation, and then once you've done it, repeat until it becomes a habit.

Let me ask you: what one decision today would make a lasting impact on your tomorrow?

At its most basic, Moses showed up. He said yes. Albeit with a little trepidation, and not a little consternation; but leave his home, lead the people and pursue his calling he did.

He Believed God

It takes courage to step out of hiddenness and believe for something new, especially when we have been hiding for many years. The gravitational pull of the familiar is often too great and it keeps us tethered to a place we, deep down, long to leave. It's like a spaceship trying to leave earth; the amount of power needed to break free is enormous, because the earth is doing everything it can to keep it grounded and stop it from casting off limitations.

When we decide to intentionally choose different thoughts, words, actions or friendship groups, the beginning will be the most challenging. It is similar to the first run after I have taken a break from running – that is always the most challenging one, because my body got lulled into the false belief that exercise was no longer necessary. But the longer I go without exercise, ironically the worse my body feels – sluggish, tired, and I begin to put on weight. It is the momentum of discipline that keeps me healthy and in the place I want to be, whether my flesh recognizes it or not. Flesh is lazy and will do whatever is necessary to avoid any type of pain or discomfort. That is the reason we must live by the spirit, not the flesh, because our spirit births life, but our flesh only breeds death.

Proverbs 23:7 (NKJV) says: 'As [a man] thinks in his heart, so is he', which means that the power of belief can be stronger than the power of reality. We see this all the time in sport when the body is screaming it is impossible, yet the mind is empowering

the marathon runner (or cyclist, swimmer, etc.) to finish the
race. You have probably heard the famous Henry Ford quote:
'Whether you think you can, or you think you can't – you're
right.'[2]

Faith chooses to believe what the word of God says over its
circumstances. We read in Mark 11:22–24:

> 'Have faith in God,' Jesus answered. 'Truly I tell you, if anyone says
> to this mountain, "Go, throw yourself into the sea," and does not
> doubt in their heart but believes that what they say will happen, it
> will be done for them. Therefore I tell you, whatever you ask for in
> prayer, believe that you have received it, and it will be yours.'

Jesus could not have made it any clearer! The discipline of faith
is what moves the mountains in our own lives. This truth is so
important to Moses' journey that it bears repeating. Moses believed God, so he left Midian and faced Pharaoh. He believed
God, so he stood at the Red Sea and did not flee in terror.
He believed God, so he approached a mountain that was terrify-
ing to see and deadly to touch. He believed
God, so he left his tent every morning to
gather the manna to eat for the day. He believed God, so he erected a Tent of Meeting
where he and God could talk. Do you see
the pattern? He believed God; he believed
God; he believed God. It was that simple –
and that difficult.

> He believed
> God; he believed
> God; he believed
> God. It was that
> simple – and that
> difficult.

It was a choice that Moses made repeatedly until he saw the
Promised Land. I use the word 'saw' because he only saw it; as a
result of choice, he didn't physically touch it. We read in Numbers 20:12: 'But the LORD said to Moses and Aaron, "Because
you did not trust in me enough to honour me as holy in the

sight of the Israelites, you will not bring this community into the land I give them.'" It seems harsh, yes, but he was the leader, and the leader is expected to be an example for those who are following.

Moses had come out of hiddenness, but he still had much to learn about holiness.

When You . . .

Not long ago I read a book by Jentzen Franklin called *Fasting: Opening the Door to a Deeper, More Intimate, More Powerful Relationship with God*.[3] It is a book worth reading (and rereading) if you want to learn more about the discipline of fasting. I gained so much from this book, but one of the greatest nuggets of truth that I took away was when Jentzen talked about Matthew 6 and the phrase 'when you'. Notice that you see the phrase three times in that chapter: 'when you give' (verse 2), 'when you pray' (verse 5) and 'when you fast' (verse 16). I doubt any of us would dispute giving or praying, yet how many of us follow the discipline of fasting as seriously as either of those two? I'll be the first to raise my hand and say that I don't . . . or at least didn't until I read this book. Therefore, I have fasted more in the past six months than in the past year altogether – and I intend to keep going!

I don't enjoy fasting. (In fact, I am in the middle of a fast right now that is due to be broken in exactly 22 minutes – not that I am counting.) Nor am I a glutton for punishment or trying to lose weight. I wouldn't even say that I understand how and why it works, but I know beyond a shadow of a doubt that it does. Spiritual strongholds can be shattered, sickness overcome, bondages broken and freedom wrought through the disciplines of prayer and fasting.

Spiritual strongholds can be shattered, sickness overcome, bondages broken and freedom wrought through the disciplines of prayer and fasting.

In his book Jentzen says: 'When you hunger for more, you will receive more.'[4] Again – *when* you. It is a choice made by us, for God. One that carries holiness within its borders, pushing past our fears, confronting our foes and releasing our future. Fasting helps us hear from heaven in a way that we can't when the noise of the everyday overwhelms our senses. Hebrews 3:7–8 reminds us not to harden our hearts, and in relation to this passage Andrew Murray says the following:

> When God [spoke] to Israel, the first thing He asked of them was a heart that did not harden itself, but that in meekness and gentleness, in tenderness and docility turned itself to listen to His voice. How much more may He claim this, now that He speaks to us in His Son. As the soil must be *broken up by the plough* and softened by the rain, so a broken, tender spirit is the first requisite for receiving blessing from God's word, or being in truth made partakers of God's grace.[5]

This isn't a book on fasting, and I couldn't possibly do it justice within a few pages, but I do want to implore us to consider adding this discipline into our spiritual lives, if this is not already happening. Perhaps, start small and with one meal only. Please don't start with an extended fast, and always consult your doctor if you have any medical conditions that could prohibit you from participating. Ask Holy Spirit what type of fast you could do (there are partial fasts, Daniel fasts, water-only fasts, etc.) and for how long.

Ensure that you have someone praying for you if this is new to you, and put aside any expectations of angel visitations within the first hour.

This is not so much about receiving as it is about releasing. Releasing our expectations, desires and control to a loving Father who knows our deepest needs and is calling out our greatest purpose. Holiness is worth pursuing; and there is no way to obtain holiness without an intentional pursuit that pushes past obstacles from the enemy, others and even our own flesh.

We must silence anything that speaks as an idol in our lives in order to hear *the* voice, the sound of the living, holy God. It is a sacrifice worth making.

Sacrifice

I have lived in England for over fifteen years. I have UK citizenship, see this as my home and feel more comfortable in this country than I do in the one where I spent the first thirty-three years of my life, but I am often asked if I miss America. Yes, of course there are still things I miss about America – my family being the most obvious. I have a young niece and nephew I won't be with as they grow up, I have siblings that I rarely see and parents who are getting older (though both look about twenty years younger than their actual age!). Only yesterday I wrote to someone that the greatest sacrifice, by far, that I have felt in moving my life overseas is missing moments with my family. American food can be bought online, but time with loved ones will only be had once, until eternity of course.

We talk about counting the cost and knowing the sacrifice before entering into something new, but can anyone truly know the sacrifice and the cost until they are asked to make it? Every parent

knows that the sleepless nights will be rough, but until you are
the one going without sleep for several weeks, months, years on
end, it is impossible to fully grasp the nuances of living at about
23% capacity.

We know that there will be sacrifices to be made when we
choose to live a debt-free lifestyle, but until we see that amazing
'70% off' deal and we don't have the cash, we can forget what
sacrifice feels like. It is easy to judge another person until we
are walking in their shoes. Or as Steve Martin says: 'Before you
criticize a man, walk a mile in his shoes. That way, when you
do criticize him, you'll be a mile away and have his shoes.'[6]

Humour aside, we can never fully grasp the depth of sacrifice Moses made to leave all and lead many. He finally had a
family of his own, he was settled in a new area where he was
living a simple life with his wife and children . . . when he was
asked to put aside his comfort for a life of wandering. And
there – in the life of wandering – was the place where Moses
developed a lifestyle of holiness.

If Moses had stayed in Midian, I doubt he would have spoken with the Lord face to face. Not only that – I would imagine
that coming off the mountain – his face shining, having encountered the glory of God for weeks at a time – would be an
experience that he would never forget. Plus, he was chosen to
be on the Mount of Transfiguration when he and Elijah spoke
with Jesus face to face. I think when we
chat to Moses in heaven, he will say the
sacrifice of comfort was worth the challenge of the unknown.

> In the kingdom,
> holiness bears
> the markings of
> sacrifice.

In the kingdom, holiness bears the mark-
ings of sacrifice.

Think of the cross as the most obvious example. Or the holy call
on the life of Mary, who sacrificed so much to birth the Saviour.

We can look at the sinful woman in Luke 7 who came out of hiding to sacrifice an alabaster jar of perfume over the feet of the Saviour. It was a holy moment, which a Pharisee, filled with judgment, completely missed.

There is much God has to say to us, if we will stay longer than is comfortable. Most of my deep, memorable encounters with God have happened after I stayed in his presence longer than intended . . . when I felt nothing, but I sought something. It is amazing, as I'm sure many of you know, when that moment arrives and suddenly the atmosphere changes. You are waiting, resting, silent, unsure of what is to come, anticipating and yet not demanding, hoping and yet trusting, when suddenly you are overcome by the glory and presence of something beyond the natural realm. It is an ecstasy that no human can give and an experience that embraces body, soul and spirit. It is a moment when time stands still and you fear to breathe, lest that moment passes. It is mortal flesh encountering eternal glory. It is a marriage of wills and a moment of wonder. His presence wraps around you and you remain frozen in wonder, not wanting to lose that perfect point in time.

Where have you sacrificed for the Lord? Have you experienced his holy touch when you have given something of value, out of deep love and obedience? Or have you left family and friends for a calling further afield?

No sacrifice goes unnoticed in the kingdom of God. Surrender and sacrifice are outward signs of inward worship, and whether the reward is now or in eternity, know that he is a rewarder of those who diligently seek him (Heb. 11:6).

But keep in mind: this pursuit still isn't about becoming perfect – it is about coming face to face with perfection himself.

For Reflection

- What would it look like for you to 'grow in favour' with God?

- 'Moses believed God.' How are you intentionally showing (or have intentionally shown) your belief in God during challenging circumstances?

- Have you ever experienced breakthrough from fasting? Is fasting a regular part of your life now? Would you like it to be?

- Think of the sacrifices that Moses made and the sacrifices you've made in your own life to follow the call of God. What similarities do you find? What differences?

17

The Big Questions

About three in the afternoon Jesus cried out
in a loud voice, 'Eli, Eli, lema sabachthani?'
(which means 'My God, my God, why have you
forsaken me?').

Matt. 27:46

'I can't believe you just asked that!' she exclaimed with tremendous shock and horror.

It was the middle of summer and I had recently moved to a lovely new flat in Bath, England. The neighbours below invited me and a few other neighbours to get together so they could meet the new girl. Another American lady, who had moved into the area a month prior to me, also joined us. We had drinks and lively chat for about an hour, when I suddenly noticed we were tiptoeing around the question of my age. Curiosity was piqued, particular questions were asked, but as they were British, nobody dared ask the obvious question.

I soon put them out of their misery and they gave the appropriate gasps of unbelief: 'Surely not! You can't possibly be forty-nine – I thought you were only thirty-five.'

Lifelong friends were made that day.

I then turned towards the other American, who had quipped that I was 'so young' and said: 'Well, how old are you then?'

You would have thought I'd politely asked if she could run naked through the garden.

The gasps, looks of horror, wine choked on and awkward silence by all the Brits was soon filled with her laughter and answer to my question, with no shame whatsoever. I knew it wouldn't be a problem because she was an American, and we feel this strange and innate freedom to ask any questions we want, intrusive or not. There were equally solicitous phrases about her youthful appearance and we all carried on as if a major breach in protocol had not just happened.

Questions are fascinating; they can open doors, shut down conversations and create intimacy. In and of themselves they are not wrong, but used in the wrong context they can be unacceptable, if not downright inappropriate. Jesus was a master of questions.

> Jesus was a master of questions.

A quick online search showed a book that proposes Jesus asked 307 questions.[1] Whether this is accurate or not, it certainly suggests he gave as many questions as answers, if not more. Jesus was comfortable with questions, and he never felt obliged to answer them. Remember him standing silent before his accusers – the ones who could have had him killed? Knowing his life was in danger created no impetus to feed their curiosity; Jesus knew they were not really seeking truth, plus he knew that his destiny was fulfilled by remaining silent. As has already been mentioned, there is a time to speak and a time to refrain from speaking.

To gain a greater understanding of how far Moses had come on his journey through the wilderness and into intimacy, we need to make a final visit to the burning bush. *Before* the role of leader was given, Moses announced: 'Here I am' (Exod. 3:4), and yet *after* he knew the plan of heaven he said: 'Who am I?' (Exod. 3:11). Promotion often unveils insecurity, and this sudden promotion caused his fears to quickly rise. Moses had a choice to make: succumb to fear or walk in obedience.

God reassures Moses that he will be with him (in other words, it doesn't matter who you are because the important factor here is who *I* am), yet Moses pushes for more information and begins outlining potential problems. He wants to make sure he has all his ducks in a row before leaving comfort behind and throwing himself head first into his calling. We tend to be like Moses – asking God copious questions and seeking 3,347 confirmations before we step forward into a new season. Why do we do this? Sometimes it is to confirm we are in the will of God, but I think more often it is because we want to maintain a level of control. Or maybe that's just me?

At any rate, I've learned that we are on a 'need to know' basis with God . . . and we don't usually need to know!

So Moses and God continue their dialogue until the point of compromise when, as we saw earlier in the book, God allowed Aaron to accompany Moses on his journey. Though Moses struggled with insecurity, we cannot ignore the fact that he had enough courage to ask questions and dialogue with the creator of the universe – albeit through a bush. The best way to know someone, aside from spending time with them, is to ask them questions and then listen – really listen.

How comfortable are you in asking God questions? If you are not in the habit of questioning God, that may be a way to deepen your intimacy with him. He may not always answer, but the seeking is just as important (if not more so) as the hearing.

Putting It into Perspective

The *Message* translation says in Psalm 145:17: 'Everything GOD does is right – the trademark on all his works is love.' I like that description: the trademark on all his works is love. In other words, if you see the fingerprint of love then you know it has originated from God, because God is love. His motives, actions and decisions will be based in love and flow from love, always. When we know love is his perspective and filter, then it helps us 'boldly approach his throne' (see Heb. 4:16) knowing he is not a father too busy with his own business to spend time with the children, but one who resembles the late President John F. Kennedy.

If you type 'President Kennedy and kids in the Oval Office' into a search engine, you will find heart-warming and poignant pictures of his very young children playing under his desk and dancing around his office area. Some of the most high-powered decisions took place in this office. It was there that President Kennedy presided over meetings and debated issues of national security, yet it was also the room in which his children were free to play, laugh and be 'Daddy's kids'. It is the perfect description of our relationship with the heavenly Father. He is Lord and King, creator of the universe and ruler of all, and yet he joyfully welcomes us to approach him with the same kind of carefreeness that the children of the president carried.

Are we comfortable playing in the throne room of heaven, so to speak? Jesus even said, 'Let the little children come', having already said in the previous chapter that we were to 'become like little children' if we wanted to enter the kingdom of heaven. A childlike trust (much different from childishness) seems fairly significant in the kingdom of God, given that it is mentioned twice by Jesus within a few chapters.

So, practically what would that look like?

Like a Child

One of the most beautiful traits of children is their innocence and their imagination. It is fascinating to play with kids and watch as they dream of adventures, create stories, believe fantasy and innocently trust the storyteller. Their trust is so deep that it allows the imagination freedom to follow a dream without throwing up practicalities or facts that would hinder it from being possible. I used to love playing imaginary games as a child, running through our woods pretending to be the Bionic Woman as my sister was Wonder Woman. Thank goodness we lived in the area – we saved those woods from many horrible attacks over the years!

If becoming childlike is mandatory for a good relationship with God, then I suggest it is something worth prioritizing. A quick look on Thesaurus.com for synonyms of 'children' brings up everything from 'ankle biter' and 'urchin' to 'little angel' and 'lamb' . . . how many of us know that they can vacillate between the two descriptions at a moment's notice! That is the way with kids; they have yet to learn how to control their emotions and so they are led by feelings and circumstances. We are meant to be like children before God, but behaviourally we are meant to mature to the point of 'eating meat' and not living on 'spiritual milk' for the rest of our lives. There is nothing cute about a 45-year-old throwing a temper tantrum or having a pity party. So, how do you act like a child and yet live like Jesus?

I don't believe the two are mutually exclusive. Living like Jesus *is* acting like a child. We know that Jesus called the Father 'Abba' in Mark 14:36 when he asked if the cup of suffering might be taken from him. In his deepest pain and before his greatest trial, Jesus drew near to his Father, addressing him as Daddy or Papa, by using the Aramaic term *Abba*. What a beautiful

Living like Jesus *is* acting like a child.

picture this paints for us when we face our own trials and suffering. So often, we pull away from God in those seasons, believing that either he is bringing harm on us, or at the very least he is allowing what he has the authority to stop in order to teach us a lesson. Those lies (perpetuated throughout the years by the enemy) will stop us from running towards the very place we can receive comfort and breakthrough – the throne room of heaven.

Jesus understood where to go in pain, and once we see the Father through his eyes, so will we. God uses our pain, but he doesn't cause it and certainly never rejoices in it.

Neither does he always explain it. The chasm caused by our lack of understanding must be covered by the bridge of faith in a loving Father. A child may not always understand a parent's decision, but maturity chooses trust over a tantrum.

> The chasm caused by our lack of understanding must be covered by the bridge of faith in a loving Father.

There is only one other person in the Bible who boldly proclaims that same descriptive term 'Abba' for the patriarch of his soul, and that is the apostle Paul – the one who initially persecuted and killed Christians. Having encountered the living God on the road to Damascus, and having spent several years being renewed in his mind and understanding of the truth, he reminds us in Romans 8:15 that we did not receive a spirit that returns us to slavery, but one that connects us to sonship – and therefore as sons and daughters we can call God 'Abba'. Paul had already alluded to this descriptive name in the book of Galatians when he tells the church in Galatia: 'Because you are his sons, God sent the Spirit of his Son into our hearts, the Spirit who calls out, "*Abba*, Father."'[2] The Spirit of his Son is the same one who can boldly, and beautifully, approach the throne of grace as a child approaches his loving Father. This is not the approach of a mature adult having an intellectual discussion with his 'stiff-upper-lipped' parent, but the relaxed and familial interaction between two who are connected – physically, spiritually and emotionally. Paul faced many hardships as a believer, but he never blamed God for those hardships; instead, he chose to press towards God's love and trust God's nature when he couldn't understand God's ways. That is maturity, and sowing trust in God will reap holiness in us.

As we talked about earlier, many of you may not have had a good relationship with your earthly father, or at least not a trusting one. Perhaps he was a good provider, but emotionally was distant. He may have been available for you to talk with, but controlling in his responses, leaving little room for disagreement. If we want to permanently leave a life of hiddenness, we must see the Father through Jesus' perspective – one who is trustworthy, safe and loving. It isn't wrong to question God, but keeping the right perspective will also help us ask the right questions. Once I remember that his nature is goodness, then I can filter my questions through the lens of love, not injustice.

> Once I remember that his nature is goodness, then I can filter my questions through the lens of love, not injustice.

Remember Job? He endured tremendous tragedy and sorrow, yet he said, at the end of the book of Job: 'I am unworthy – how can I reply to you? I put my hand over my mouth.'[3] In other words, I realize that my humanity cannot be compared to your divinity . . . and I choose to trust divinity.

At this moment there is an open invitation to the throne room of his presence, and all who go there will find that as they linger, they will receive far more than they bring: 'Blessed and fortunate and happy and spiritually prosperous (in that state in which the born-again child of God enjoys His favor and salvation) are those who hunger and thirst for righteousness (uprightness and right standing with God), for they shall be completely satisfied!'[4]

For Reflection

- Do you tend to ask more questions or give more answers? What would it look like for you to lean more towards the other direction?

- Are your questions to God usually based on insecurity or on curiosity? Are they designed to know him more or to help you more?

- In what ways do you feel 'childlike' when approaching God?

- Would you be comfortable calling God 'Abba'? Why or why not?

18

Glory

Then Moses said, 'Now show me your glory.'
Exod. 33:18

There was a popular song many years ago with the appealing title 'Friend of God'. It talked about the friendship between God and humanity, implying surprise that a mighty God would be mindful of mere human beings. It was a very simple song, continuously repeating the idea that we are God's friend. I remember driving in my car belting it out at the top of my lungs, rejoicing in the fact that I was on a first-name basis with the creator of the universe himself!

It really is quite extraordinary to think that while God is talking with me, he can simultaneously be ministering to a dying woman in China and giving direction to a young man in California – each feeling they are the only one holding his attention at that moment.

That is what a real friend does; when you are together, they let you know that you are their priority. Intimately acquainted with your strengths and weaknesses, they also love you without pressure to change or be anyone other than the best version of you that you can be. Those types of friends are very special and those friendships can take years to cultivate – doing the

journey through life's ups and downs, loving you for who you
are, not for who you were. Do you have this type of friendship
with God?

I believe it is possible for everyone to experience an extraordinary, deep friendship with God, but as we see in James 2:
21–23 it takes both faith and obedience:

> Was not our father Abraham considered righteous for what he did
> when he offered his son Isaac on the altar? You see that his faith
> and his actions were working together, and his faith was made
> complete by what he did. And the scripture was fulfilled that says,
> 'Abraham believed God, and it was credited to him as righteous-
> ness,' and he was called God's friend.

Moses believed God, as Abraham did. He took risks, stepped
out in faith and pushed beyond his insecurities and 'need to
know' in order to behold what others had not seen – the face
of God.

Face to Face

At this point, I want to deal with what could be a confusing
piece of Scripture, but one that is essential to this journey.
Notice the apparent contradiction between these two verses
from Exodus chapter 33 (emphasis mine):

> *The LORD would speak to Moses face to face*, as one speaks to a
> friend. Then Moses would return to the camp, but his young
> assistant Joshua son of Nun did not leave the tent.

Exod. 33:11

'But,' he said, '*you cannot see my face, for no one may see me and live.*'

Exod. 33:20

In verse 11 we see Moses and God speaking face to face, but nine verses later God seems to contradict himself by saying Moses cannot see his face and live. How can both of these be accurate? I am slightly hesitant to step into this discussion as it carries a much deeper theological discussion than this book is designed to give, but I did not want to avoid what, to me, is an obvious question when I think of face-to-face encounters with God. If you are interested in a much more in-depth understanding, I would encourage you to do further research on this subject. You can read commentaries online, and The Discovery Bible[1] is an excellent tool for doing further study as a layperson to understand the Hebrew and Greek and gain a deeper understanding of the Scriptures.

I want to highlight one brief paragraph from Scottish theologian Alexander Maclaren, who gives a thought-provoking, profound explanation around the heart-cry of Moses to see God's glory:

Moses' prayer sounds presumptuous, but it was heard unblamed, and granted in so far as possible. It was a venial error – if error it may be called – that a soul, touched with the flame of divine love, should aspire beyond the possibilities of mortality. At all events, it was a fault in which he has had few imitators. *Our* desires keep but too well within the limits of the possible. The precise meaning of the petition must be left undetermined. Only this is clear, that it was something far beyond even that face-to-face intercourse which he had had, as well as beyond that vision granted to the elders. If we are to take 'glory' in its usual sense, it would mean the material symbol of God's presence, which shone at the heart of the pillar, and dwelt afterwards between the cherubim, but probably we must attach a loftier meaning to it here, and rather think of what we should call the uncreated and infinite divine essence. Only do not let us make Moses talk like a metaphysician or a theological professor. Rather we should hear in his cry the voice of a soul thrilled through and through with the astounding consciousness of God's favour, blessed with love-gifts in answered prayers, and yearning for more of that light which it feels to be life.[2]

Maclaren goes on to bring a distinction between the glory and goodness of God, pointing out what God *will* give (goodness, graciousness, compassion) as opposed to what his divinity must hold back. This was not about God being stingy and playing hard-to-get with Moses, but rather a God of love entrusting all that was possible to satisfy a man hungry for divine presence yet bound to earth's humanity. Moses was limited to the degree that any mortal human being is, when associating with an immortal and omniscient God, as he had not yet embraced his glorified body, which is yet to come at Christ's return.[3]

Dr Gary Hill explains it this way: 'We need a glorified body to see more of God or we would perish . . . so I think on this discussion about "seeing him and live" it isn't so much the particular word [live] . . . as the manifest unveiling and that we have to see a backside until we receive our glorified bodies.'[4]

God gives as much as he can while we are in our temporary, earthly home, but he is still limited on how much of him can be revealed. With that being said, the amount he *can* show us far exceeds the depth of our desire. Ask for more. Cry out for more. Desire more. As a diamond reflects the light, revealing new angles of its brilliance with every turn, so does God display new aspects of his glory with each touch of his presence. There is a powerful paradox in the kingdom that as we seek him we will find him, but as we find him we deepen our desire to seek him.

> Ask for more.
> Cry out for more.
> Desire more.

With that in mind, let's return to verse 11 and the Hebrew word *panim*, meaning 'face'. *Panim* can also be used for 'presence', first appearing in the second verse of the Bible: 'Now the earth was formless and empty, darkness was over the surface of the deep, and the Spirit of God was hovering over the waters.'[5] The Hebrew word for 'surface' is the same word for 'face'; in other words, the *face* of the deep was darkened at creation. This reveals that it isn't a literal face, but an idea that conveys an atmosphere or area, rather than one specific set of human features.

From the beginning of time (in Genesis) throughout eternity (in Revelation), God's presence has always been and always will be. Because of the cross of Jesus Christ, we have the hope of joining all the saints and the great 'I AM' (Exod. 3:14) in the beautiful union of the Bride and her Bridegroom. The King has already won the battle, and on that day the King will win his bride. The war will be finished and the enemy cast out, silenced for eternity. In our day-to-day

> The King has already won the battle, and on that day the King will win his bride.

struggles it is good to remember that we will see this wonder with our own eyes – we *will* be part of this end-time extravaganza. Imagine that day: such love. Such wonder. Such beauty. Such *celebration*!

Yet our time of preparation is now, so will you – like Moses – draw near, push past your fears, seek more of the Lord and recklessly pursue holiness?

Seated with Him

God reminds Moses that although he encountered God in the tent (and the bush), he should not presume on or misjudge their relationship – God is still God and Moses is still human:

> And the LORD said, 'I will cause all my goodness to pass in front of you, and I will proclaim my name, the LORD, in your presence. I will have mercy on whom I will have mercy, and I will have compassion on whom I will have compassion. But,' he said, 'you cannot see my face, for no one may see me and live.'[6]

This makes the cross even more amazing! Now through the blood of Jesus Christ we are *allowed* to approach his throne of grace and seek his face (presence) with as much hunger and desire as we like. I wonder if we have fully understood this *invitation* to sit in heavenly places with him, while yet on earth? In other words, distance carries no real separation in this relationship; though we are apart physically, by the spirit we sit together.

We see this vividly in Colossians 2:9–10 where The Passion Translation says: 'For he is the complete fullness of deity living in human form. And our own completeness is now found in him. We are completely filled *with God* as Christ's fullness overflows within us. He is the Head of every kingdom and authority in the universe!'

We are thoroughly filled with God, equipped and emboldened with all the power and authority Christ himself walked with on the earth. That is our heritage and our right standing before God at this very moment. Heaven is not the time we will need to exercise our authority against the enemy – that is our privilege *now*!

I want to live in the fullness of dominion, wisdom, power and knowledge that I have been given while I am here on earth – not squander the blood of Jesus and the cross of Christ by remaining defeated when in reality victorious.

Moses was allowed to be in the presence of the Lord for a period of time, but there was a limit to that relationship because there was a limit to Moses' holiness. He still had to make sacrifices for his sins, whereas we are under the new covenant and have had our sins atoned for once and for all through Jesus Christ. This has opened a new way for us to approach the throne of heaven, and we are seen by God as holy and blameless because of Jesus' sacrifice on our behalf. Therefore, surely our relationship and intimacy with the Father has the potential to go beyond what he had with Moses, as God is no respecter of persons?

Of course, we still have the beautiful privilege of repentance for those times we have sinned, but we do this knowing that our sin has already been atoned for through the blood of Jesus. Therefore, we can come boldly before the throne of grace, not as 'sinners saved by grace', but as fully loved and accepted children of God ready to receive love, grace, forgiveness and freedom, as seen in Hebrews 10:19–23:

Therefore, brothers and sisters, since we have confidence to enter the Most Holy Place by the blood of Jesus, by a new and living way opened for us through the curtain, that is, his body, and since we have a great priest over the house of God, let us draw near to God with a sincere heart and with the full assurance that faith brings, having our hearts sprinkled to cleanse us from a guilty conscience and having our bodies washed with pure water. Let us hold unswervingly to the hope we profess, for he who promised is faithful.

Moses could experience a level of God's glory and presence in the tent and on the mountain, but we can experience a fuller measure through the blood of Christ, as we seek by faith to live the abundant life here on earth. Amazing!

With that being said, as was mentioned above, only in heaven will we experience the *fullness* of God's glory – a display of power and beauty unlike anything we could experience here on earth. We anticipate that union with bated breath and passionate expectation, as described in Revelation 21:1–7:

> We anticipate that union with bated breath and passionate expectation.

Then I saw 'a new heaven and a new earth,' for the first heaven and the first earth had passed away, and there was no longer any sea. I saw the Holy City, the new Jerusalem, coming down out of heaven from God, prepared as a bride beautifully dressed for her husband. And I heard a loud voice from the throne saying, 'Look! God's dwelling-place is now among the people, and he will dwell with them. They will be his people, and God himself will be with them and be their God. "He will wipe every tear from their eyes. There will be no more death" or mourning or crying or pain, for the old order of things has passed away.'

He who was seated on the throne said, 'I am making everything new!' Then he said, 'Write this down, for these words are trustworthy and true.'

He said to me: 'It is done. I am the Alpha and the Omega, the Beginning and the End. To the thirsty I will give water without cost from the spring of the water of life. Those who are victorious will inherit all this, and I will be their God and they will be my children.'

For Reflection

- How would you describe your friendship with God?

- What would it look like for you to have a 'face-to-face' relationship with God? Does that excite you or scare you?

- If Moses could get that close to God before Jesus' sacrifice on the cross, what difference do you think the blood of Jesus makes for us to approach the throne room of heaven?

- If you were Joshua, would you have wanted to enter the tent? Would you have stayed?

19

The Clue Is in the Cleft

*O my dove, in the clefts of the rock, in the cran-
nies of the cliff, let me see your face, let me hear
your voice, for your voice is sweet, and your face
is lovely.*

Song 2:14 ESV

In John 17 we read what is called the 'high-priestly prayer' and
in verses 20–23 (ESV) we see Jesus speak about unity between
believers and the Godhead:

I do not ask for these only, but also for those who will believe
in me through their word, that they may all be one, just as you,
Father, are in me, and I in you, that they also may be in us, so that
the world may believe that you have sent me. The glory that you
have given me I have given to them, that they may be one even
as we are one, I in them and you in me, that they may become
perfectly one, so that the world may know that you sent me and
loved them even as you loved me.

I have seen the opposite too many times in ministry: misunderstanding, hurt, judgment and division. The result is rarely

positive and unfortunately there are casualties on all sides. To be honest, using the word 'side' within a Christian context grieves my heart, and I believe it grieves the Father's heart even more. We are meant to be unified, loving, supportive and championing one another to become more Christlike as we live for the cause of Christ. So why do we find so many church splits and leadership crises within the Christian world?

There are several factors at work when division occurs, not the least of which is a very real enemy of our souls. The Bible is clear that we fight 'not against flesh and blood, but against the rulers, against the authorities, against the powers of this dark world' (Eph. 6:12), and yet when it comes to everyday hurt there is often a human face on the other end of a painful accusation or offending comment.

> When it comes to everyday hurt there is often a human face on the other end of a painful accusation or offending comment.

For a moment, let's imagine coming in the opposite spirit. Unity could be described as 'two parts coming together as one', involving connection, cooperation and creation. This also applies to the body of Christ. If we want to walk unified then we must connect with one another beyond our comfort zone and cooperate beyond our theological differences – creating something far greater together than apart.

I am not saying we must agree on all points, nor am I watering down the quest to understand deep truths and uphold spiritual laws. Compromising beliefs is not necessary to cooperate as believers. Of course there will be crucial issues on which we may never agree, but should that stop us from loving one another? Is that a reason to publicly humiliate and tear down another's convictions? We never see Jesus leading a charge to personally humiliate the Pharisees, digging into their history so that he can flaunt their every sin. That is what the *religious* leaders were doing, and they were condemned for it, as seen in the beautiful example of the woman caught in adultery, who, let's remember, was allowed to break free from her accusers and step into a new life of grace, forgiveness and lack of judgment. Jesus united himself with sinners by sharing their food and conversation, while also maintaining connection with those Jewish leaders who were seeking truth – for example, by meeting them in the dark and answering their questions about being born again.

Again, this does not mean accepting as true something we believe is sinful, but it does mean that, while we stand our ground against evil, we refuse evil ground in our own hearts.

This isn't easy, but it is possible and we must do it – because a tempting alternative to unity is division, and division will never heal a relationship, let alone a church or a nation.

There Is a Place

> *Then the LORD said, 'There is a place near me where you may stand on a rock.'*
>
> *Exod. 33:21*

The further we remove ourselves from hiding, the greater our capacity to connect. If we require continual affirmation of our worth or separate ourselves by means of a self-protective shield, we perpetuate the plan of the enemy, which is always division. As we saw in the first chapter, it started in

> The further we remove ourselves from hiding, the greater our capacity to connect.

the Garden of Eden when Satan planted seeds of doubt in order to grow a harvest of disunity, and it worked – for a time.

But the enemy's time is limited, and regardless of his efforts, the cross of Jesus Christ broke down every barrier, tore apart the veil of separation and created a bridge for the rejected to be welcomed home. The work may have been finished on the cross, but a lie still hovers in many hearts across the earth: millions of people believe they cannot approach a holy God, and sadly the judgment of Christians has often done more harm than good in combating this myth.

The Bible says that others will know we are believers by our love, but that love is muted if they hear us through our judgment. That is why standing in grace, on the rock of our salvation, is so important. Moses declared this in the desert when he said in Deuteronomy 32:4:

> The Bible says that others will know we are believers by our love, but that love is muted if they hear us through our judgment.

He is the Rock, his works are perfect,
    and all his ways are just.
A faithful God who does no wrong,
    upright and just is he.

The Hebrew word for 'Rock' (*sûr*) is described as 'what can not be moved, removed, or ignored; a refuge affording enduring, unshakable protection because of its sure foundation (base) making it immoveable'.[1]

In her book *Adamant*, Lisa Bevere says: 'The Rock is our strength, our sure footing in a world littered with gravel. Jesus is our stronghold when our enemies want to put us in a stranglehold. The Rock is our rescue, safeguard, and armor of defense.'[2]

In a world filled with division, judgment, constant change and movable truths, Christ is our immovable refuge and constant source of safety. Running to him reveals that we are no longer hiding out of sin, but recipients of his grace. The desert was filled with brokenness, insecurity and confusion, while the rock symbolizes freedom, safety and vision.

We will never fully take refuge on the mountain of grace if we don't stop hiding in our desert of shame. I have discovered, alongside Moses, that when invited there . . . the mountain is the safest place to go.

Cleft

I will never forget one particular morning. It was during a difficult season, with signs of division encircling me like vultures looking for food – people saying hurtful comments, untruths being perpetuated and accusations rife. My Bible reading took me to Exodus 33, one of my favourite chapters, and I read verse 22 where the cleft of a rock is mentioned. I decided to look up the word 'cleft', and one of the definitions was something like 'split in two or separate'. I felt the nudge of Holy Spirit reminding me that Moses was *deliberately* put into the cleft. That's when I saw it: our place of division, amid the confusion and pain, can ultimately be a refuge of safety – because it was there the goodness of God visited. In that moment the sweet whisper of heaven spoke to my heart and let me know that through this hurtful season, if I remained in the cleft, division would not be my undoing. On the contrary, it would open the heavens for an outpouring of God's goodness.

As the heart of a parent hurts when their children are estranged from one another, relational breakdowns in the body of Christ must grieve the heart of God. I have not experienced divorce in my life or immediate family, but I have seen it play out in the lives of those close to me. It carries shame, misunderstanding, deep pain and a great sense of loss. Those of you who have walked this road will articulate it far greater than I could. When you have surrendered your heart to another, trusted them with the deepest and most vulnerable areas of your life, and yet had them use those secrets against you (or at the very least take those secrets outside your ability to guard them), fear can rise on so many levels. In this situation it would be difficult not to create barriers around yourself that are impenetrable to others, let alone the Lord.

How do you trust again? *Do* you trust again? These are questions only love, time and personal choices can answer. Moses understood the sense of frustration – and isolation – when it seems that all you have worked for is lost. Remember, he had left the comfort of familiarity to take up the call of leadership. He had confronted Pharaoh, endured relentless complaining from a few million people, fasted for forty days and nights (twice), climbed a mountain (at the age of 80+) and witnessed the people he loved reject God by worshipping a golden idol.[3]

Even worse, his brother, who had been his partner and mouthpiece, was lured into the Israelites' deception by planning the creation of the golden idol. When Moses descended the mountain and saw their idol worship, his temper flared; he broke the tablets bearing the Ten Commandments and ground their man-made idol to a powder, which he forced them to drink. After confronting his brother, he was met with the ridiculous story that the calf had magically appeared out of the fire after Aaron had thrown in a few gold earrings. Really, Aaron, that's the best you could do?

Quickly, Moses regained control by asking whoever was for the Lord to come stand by him. The Levites joined his side and they were given orders to kill their brothers, friends and neighbours – about three thousand people died that day. Idolatry and rebellion created a division that could not be tolerated, and as one would remove a cancer destroying a healthy body, that day the cancerous rebellion was removed from their midst.

Imagine how Moses felt as he climbed the mountain after seeing three thousand people he had led and loved being slaughtered on account of their rebellion. As a leader he must have wondered if he could have avoided this in some way – was it his fault? God understood his pain of rejection, and soon Moses discovers that on the mountain, isolated and alone, is where the Lord's goodness mingles with our grief. Inviting God into our suffering and division allows him to work all things together for our good . . . and all things means *all* things.

It helps to remember that our lives are like a puzzle, and the totality is not based around one piece but is a progressive picture woven together over time. Some are larger pieces than others, but none represent the whole. As our personalities are unique and impossible to fully comprehend – made up of pieces such as past experiences, DNA, choices and preferences – so is the picture of our lives. Therefore, when there is a piece of the puzzle that is hard (impossible) to comprehend, we can choose to surrender it to heaven, asking our Father to enhance the beauty of our story through the pieces of our heart.

Brokenness becomes beauty when strategically placed by the hand of God. One of the most breathtaking mosaics I have ever seen is in St Mark's Basilica in Venice, Italy. The opulence and beauty of the design literally left me speechless as I spent

> Brokenness becomes beauty when strategically placed by the hand of God.

many minutes in silence – staring – awestruck at the creation. Yet if you pulled out one piece on its own, or even a few pieces, you would only see brokenness.

It helps to trust the Creator when we don't understand the creation – not out of duty, but from a place of love. Love for who he is, not for what he brings to us or how he answers our prayers. It is one of the most difficult parts of our Christian walk and one that calls on the deep places of maturity.

Where is your cleft in the rock? Is the Lord calling you to find peace in a place of division, perhaps from years ago? Any area of unforgiveness or offence will create separation in our hearts. However justified we may feel about the anger we carry, there is no justification in Scripture to hold on to offence and bitterness or to withhold forgiveness. One cannot remain in offence and have deep intimacy with God – it is impossible. Forgiveness does not mean accepting back into our lives some-one who is unhealthy or abusive, but it does mean unhooking ourselves from their deception by clearing our own heart of any roots of bitterness or offence.

Not all broken relationships are meant to be restored, but they can all be redeemed – as we let them go, placing those memories into our mosaic.

Holiness

> *Make every effort to live in peace with everyone and to be holy; without holiness no one will see the Lord.*
>
> *Heb. 12:14*

Having spoken to the Lord face to face, Moses encountered holiness up close and personal. As we said in the last chap-ter, it's amazing to think that this was before the resurrection of Christ, so there was a deep level of holiness he walked in

without the indwelling empowerment of Holy Spirit. Not perfection – holiness.

Before we forget, Moses was far from perfect. He spent forty
years in Midian because of his temper and he did not enter the
Promised Land (during his earthly life) due to his short fuse.
He struggled with insecurity and had to learn patience. But his
heart for God never seemed to waver, and there was a purity
that drew the presence of God and won over the hearts of other
people, which is something worth emulating.

How hungry are we for holiness – a desire for God that takes
us beyond sinful flesh and unanswered questions? A desire that
chooses time with him over the tug of the duvet, and sets aside
the pleasure of food in the pursuit of his presence? When was
the last time you fell to your knees in absolute awe – overcome
with his majesty and enamoured of his glory? How often do
you look to the skies, seas or hills and thank him for his creation? Does your body physically hunger for his presence and
your spirit long to be saturated in his glory?

My humanity often obstructs my desire for holiness, yet this
morning I found myself prostrate – crying out for more of his
presence – desiring to touch him in a way I have not yet experienced. Admittedly, those times are not often for me, and as I
write this book I am convicted that there is more . . . so much
more. More to be experienced, learned, touched, felt, understood and known.

In this generation, we mustn't let division be the definition
of the church; we were created for something greater, and as we
will see in the final few chapters, what we choose now is the
legacy we will leave tomorrow.

For Reflection

- Is it possible to experience the unity of heaven here on earth?

- What can Moses' journey teach us about what to do in times of division and misunderstanding, and how to maintain holiness when confronted with heartache?

- In what ways is the Lord a 'Rock' in your life, as described in Deuteronomy 32:4?

- How have you seen your broken pieces become a beautiful mosaic?

- Have you sought to know God as intimately as you know your spouse or closest friend? If not, what would that look like for you?

Part Six

For All Eternity

20

The Cloud

*By day the L*ORD *went ahead of them in a pillar
of cloud to guide them on their way and by night
in a pillar of fire to give them light, so that they
could travel by day or night.*

Exod. 13:21

One of my favourite box sets to watch has to be one that follows a mother/daughter story and takes place in a fictional
American town called Stars Hollow. The theme song is a re-
make of an old Carole King song, describing the strength of
a mother/daughter relationship in which they will always be
together – one following wherever the other wants to go. It got
me thinking: *Can I say to the Lord with honesty and conviction:
where you lead, I will follow?*

It is a bold statement because the Lord
will lead us to places we didn't know we
wanted to go . . . yet bring us into places we
could not imagine our lives without. First,
we must be able to hear and discern what
he is saying.

I find it interesting that so many people
choose to lead their lives separated from God,

> The Lord will lead
> us to places we
> didn't know we
> wanted to go . . .
> yet bring us into
> places we could
> not imagine our
> lives without.

when he is the one who knows *why* he created them and the purpose behind their lives:

> For you created my inmost being; you knit me together in my mother's womb. I praise you because I am fearfully and wonderfully made; your works are wonderful, I know that full well. My frame was not hidden from you when I was made in the secret place, when I was woven together in the depths of the earth. Your eyes saw my unformed body; all the days ordained for me were written in your book before one of them came to be.[1]

Of course, it isn't all 'bells and whistles', and life will always throw a few curve balls our way, but the heart of a loving, earthly father is that his children are content, fulfilled and at peace. Your heavenly Father is no different.

So, when the Lord spoke to me in 2002 and said: 'Your time in Michigan is done and I'm sending you to England', I knew his offer came with a choice: would I follow where he was leading?

To better understand my decision, we must rewind to a time much earlier than that – 1991 to be exact.

Supernatural in the Supermarket

It was approaching spring and I was soon to graduate from Hope College,[2] yet I was still undecided on what to do. At this point in my life even my goals have goals, but growing up I was never the kid who knew exactly what she wanted. I was the daydreamer, the lover of romance and happy endings, the carefree drama student and the adventurer. I wanted to become an actress so that I could 'be' many different people over my lifetime.

The thought of only being Jen Baker seemed rather boring to me; what if I was meant to be a pilot, a barista, a businesswoman or – more importantly – a famous spy ('The name is Baker . . . Jen Baker'). How could I fulfil all of those dreams in one lifetime? The logical solution: become an actress. To me, that seemed the best way to 'suck the marrow out of life', quoting Henry David Thoreau, and truly get as much out of this journey as possible. Thankfully, the Lord intervened.

Zig Ziglar says: 'If you aim at nothing you will hit it every time.'[3] This soon proved true in my own life. I had become a Christian at the age of 19 and the theatre world soon clashed with my newfound beliefs, but if I wasn't going to be an actress, then what would I do? I had always felt a calling to be on the stage and my mind was filled with countless ways this could happen, but nothing felt right. As a result, I found myself aimless and wandering – terrified of missing my purpose as graduation approached with no exit strategy. It was then that I heard the audible voice of God in the supermarket.

No, it wasn't over the loudspeaker in aisle two. I was standing in the queue holding my noodles when I thought a man behind me was speaking near my ear. I literally jumped and swung around, expecting to see a bloke breathing down my neck. But to my confusion, there was not another person in sight . . . literally, not one. Turning around again, clutching my noodles for protection, I heard the same voice, this time speaking more slowly and with tremendous authority and intention: 'I am calling you into full-time ministry.'

I turned as if in slow motion, somehow knowing I would find myself staring at a vacant store. Standing there, I wondered what it all meant. This was a Saturday morning and I was just a girl shopping for noodles – I certainly wasn't expecting a heavenly visitation. Suddenly, I had an inkling of what Moses might have felt like when the bush would not stop burning. Ordinary Saturday this was not; the till[4] had just become an altar.

Could I leave my desires and dreams behind? I knew God was asking that of me; I don't know how I knew, but I knew. If I obeyed, it meant laying aside every hope and dream I wanted in order to take up the call of God on my life – *before* knowing

> My voice was muted out of fear, but my heart squeaked 'yes' out of faith.

what that call entailed. My voice was muted out of fear, but my heart squeaked 'yes' out of faith.

I didn't realize it at the time, but in that moment I began to 'follow the cloud'. I use that phrase quite regularly now and by it I mean 'follow where the Lord is leading'. As Moses and the Israelites followed the cloud by day and fire by night, so I believe he leads us in much the same way. There are signs that we can follow, and when we recognize them we have a choice: go or stay?

My prayer is that through the reading of this book you have been drawn towards a journey of holiness and a retreat from hiddenness – choosing to take risks, believing that his leading always draws us nearer to his heart of love and purpose over our lives.

In the Old Testament the cloud always moved with intention, was led by the Lord and involved a choice by the people. As we near the end of our journey, I want us to think about our own lives and how willing we are to follow the cloud when it moves.

For me, that began by saying no to a pair of socks.

Can You Hear Me?

Some time after my supermarket encounter, I went into a store to buy some socks and as I was about to carry them to the counter

I heard Holy Spirit say: 'Don't buy the socks.' I stood confused, and slightly amused, that the Lord would care about socks. We bantered back and forth for a few minutes and then I left the store – without my socks. In the car I asked the Lord why he cared if I bought socks, when clearly it was a need and I had the money. He said that he wanted to know if I would listen to him and obey in the little things. If I hadn't walked in obedience to the little desires of my heart, how would he know that he could trust me with the bigger ones?

I could have left that day with socks and possibly I would still be where I am today, but I don't think so – because every moment of disobedience makes it easier to disregard the voice of heaven in the future. Hearing the voice of God is a novelty to some and a normality to others. There are those people who chat to him all the time, and others who say it has been years since they heard his voice and even then they were uncertain it was from heaven. Most of us fall somewhere in-between the two – learning, listening and practising – hoping that we are hearing correctly, yet at times mixed with a twinge of doubt.

I would suggest that we hear him more than we think we do; the voice of God is speaking all the time – through others, nature, music, the Bible and circumstance. The challenge is not his silence, but our hearing. A.W. Tozer says: 'The Bible is not only a book which was once spoken, but a book which is now speaking.'[5]

We cannot claim God is silent if we fail to read the Bible on a consistent basis – that is not fair to a loving God who wrote the book *in order to* speak to us. His word speaks to us all the time; every scripture promise is speaking to our lives and personal circumstances. The lessons we can learn from those who have lived before us in both the Old and New Testaments are all life lessons to us; and the Holy Spirit who breathed life into the pages is the same Holy Spirit who is with us right now at this moment, bringing understanding, conviction and clarity.

There are a myriad of ways to read the Bible: verse by verse, by topic, by book, following a year's reading plan, the gospels only, the words in red only, and many more. Perhaps that is part of our problem; as we can feel overwhelmed by the continual stream of information in today's world, so we can be overcome by the 1,189 chapters staring back at us every time we sit down to read Scripture. We think that it all seems too much and we probably won't understand it anyway, so best wait until Sunday when we get fed by the sermon and hope that meal will satisfy our hunger for another week.

Christians cannot live in today's world on 'sound-bite Christianity' as it will never sustain or mature us to do our journey well. To expect someone else to define where our cloud is moving is lazy Christianity. Yes, get

> We cannot live in today's world on 'sound-bite Christianity'.

outside counsel when you feel God is leading you somewhere, and yes, trust your leaders as they often see what we cannot, but always – *always* – be led by peace.

Peace

One of my favourite verses is Colossians 3:15 which says: 'Let the peace of Christ rule in your hearts, since as members of one body you were called to peace. And be thankful.'

That is such a beautiful verse! You may have heard that the word 'rule' actually means 'to act as an umpire' – it means to judge whether something is in or out. Learning how to be led by peace is crucial to the believer, because there are so many things trying to steal our peace in the natural realm. The enemy cannot take our peace; he can affect our minds and attack our physical bodies, but he cannot steal our peace, unless we give him licence to do so. That is the reason why, in the midst of the storm on Lake Galilee, Jesus was asleep in the boat. God had told them they would go to the other side, so there was no doubt in his mind that is where they were headed, storm or not. Jesus' peace came from his trust in the Father, not in the navigational skills of the disciples.

One of the most beautiful ways to know God's peace and to recognize God's leading is to rest in God's presence. Being still is a lost art today, as a sound-bite generation grows uneasy with silence for any length of time. But in times of silence, God often speaks the loudest.

When was the last time you sat in silence before the Lord, simply resting? Quietly. In peace. Maybe you should put the book down now, make yourself a hot drink, sit down in quietness, take three very long and deep breaths and . . . rest.

Wait.

Pause.

Feels good, doesn't it?

Stillness allows us to see cloud formation. Remember the story in 1 Kings 18 where Elijah has just defeated the prophets of Baal and God won a great victory, then he climbs Mount Carmel, clearly exhausted from the recent battle? It was there he told his servant to go look at the sea for the coming storm, but the servant returned with a negative report, saying he could see nothing. Seven times Elijah had him return, until the servant finally says, 'A cloud as small as a man's hand is rising from the sea', at which point Elijah tells him to get a move on because the storm is coming.

The cloud moved both: a seeking servant and a waiting Moses.

Rachel Held Evans puts it this way: 'Faith isn't about having everything figured out ahead of time; faith is about following the quiet voice of God *without* having everything figured out ahead of time.'[6]

The cloud won't explain where you are going, but it will point you in the direction you are meant to follow.

> The cloud won't explain where you are going, but it will point you in the direction you are meant to follow.

Follow the Sound

Recently I was watching a nature programme and this particular episode featured the penguins (a personal favourite of mine). I can't remember which breed of penguin, but the filming started the day they all gathered together to find a partner. It was chaos. The guys are trying to entice the girls, and the girls are choosing which one looks good to them.

Seriously, ladies? They all look exactly the same.

Finally, a mate is chosen, some 'interaction' occurs, and presto – a little penguin egg is created. It is at that point that the girls take off to find some food and leave the guys to look after the eggs. Once they return the eggs have hatched and the chick is hungry; this will be Mum's first introduction to her baby. But before she arrives she has to find her partner in the midst of *thousands* of other penguins . . . each one looking *exactly* like his neighbour. The only way to find him? Listen for his sound.

Every penguin has a unique sound, and when the ladies are seen from afar the guys start going crazy, all yelling and screaming, each one hoping that his voice stands out amid the other thousand guys happy to see their woman arriving home with the groceries. Following the sound is what leads the mother penguin to her baby, mate and new season.

Just follow the sound. What is screaming for your attention right now? What are the thousand other voices or distractions pulling you away from hearing the voice of the Lord? Can we make *his* sound our most important sound – the Lord calling us to him in the morning, wooing us to spend time with him in prayer and worship. Will we allow his voice to override the din of the world's demands on our time?

It might mean waking fifteen minutes (or an hour) early, refusing to look at the phone until you've had your quiet time, changing the settings on your phone so that you don't see any alerts until a certain time of day, or refusing yourself coffee if you look at your phone before your Bible (gasp!). It might mean shutting off the television in the evening and curling up with your journal and Bible, or taking part in that church Bible study instead of catching up on the latest TV show.

If we think hearing him will be difficult, then it will be difficult. Alternatively, if we believe we can hear his voice, we will. John 10:27 says: 'My sheep listen to my voice; I know them, and they follow me.'

And Jeremiah 29:13 says: 'You will seek me and find me when you seek me with all your heart.'

He loves to speak to us, so seek his face, ask him questions and listen for his response. If you don't hear anything, be patient and try again. Eventually you will hear him speak and what he says could be life-changing, not only for you but for those who are following behind.

For Reflection

- Have you ever had to 'follow the cloud' in your life? What was the outcome?

- Do you find it easy to hear God? How have you developed in that area?

- How have you learned to have peace in the midst of a storm?

- What 'sound' do you hear from heaven?

21

The Next Generation

The LORD would speak to Moses face to face, as one speaks to a friend. Then Moses would return to the camp, but his young assistant Joshua son of Nun did not leave the tent.

Exod. 33:11

Scene: we're all building blocks on the floor; Dorothy is, apparently, the one in charge of the build site.

Dorothy: 'Mom, those blocks don't go next.'
Me (choosing a different block to go next): 'How about this one?'
Dorothy: 'No! Mom! Those are the wrong blocks! Do you know what listening is?'

The above is a post from my sister-in-law's social media page[1] after a conversation with my extremely precious (and precocious) 4-year-old niece, Dorothy. Normally her parents will kindly ask her if she has 'put on her listening ears' when she seems to be ignoring their instructions, but Dorothy's style has taken what they say and modified it into something a bit more . . . direct!

The next generation is watching us whether we want them to or not. They are watching the church to see how we respond, *if* we respond and to what degree we respond. They are judging our motives, words, compassion and acceptance; for post-millennials, anything less than complete inclusion is anathema to their sensitive natures.

In a world of social media, where everyone can have a voice, often the voice of faith is silenced by the voice of the masses, the media, the victim, the popular . . . you fill in the blank. Fear of offending has often become fear of speaking. To hold a view different from that of your friends might mean social media exclusion or a

> Fear of offending has often become fear of speaking.

rapid decline in the number of social media 'friends'. It is a fickle system, which sees truth bowing down to fake news on a regular basis.

Moses' lifestyle of holiness set an example for those who followed – namely Joshua, his successor, who famously declared: 'As for me and my household we will serve the Lord.'

'Legacy' can be an overused word, but if we want to fully eradicate hiddenness and embody holiness, then we will intentionally see our relationship with the Lord move beyond our lives to impact the next generation.

The Death of Faith

On more than one occasion, we have seen Moses 'stand in the gap' for his generation and the generations to follow. He was willing to sacrifice his family, future, comfort and comfort zone in order to see freedom for those he would never meet. As seen in this quote by Andrew Murray, that is the power of legacy:

There is no power on earth that can stand before the power of faith, because the power of faith is the power of God working in us . . . Selfishness is the death of faith. *How can ye believe who take honour one of another?* As long as we seek to be strong in faith, for the sake of our own comfort and goodness, and the possession of power, even if we dream of using it all for others, when once we obtain it, we shall fail. It is the soul that at once, in its weakness, gives itself up for the sake of God and others, that will find in that self-sacrifice the need and the right to claim God's mighty help.[2]

Faith was never meant to set its borders around our dreams alone; it was designed to unlock the dreams of others. We journey out of hiddenness, to help others find holiness. By seeing a generation fully abandoned in trust, unbridled in compassion and resolute in faith, we will help secure a foundation that can take future generations to the realm of the miraculous and beyond any ceilings of doubt and unbelief this generation has set up.

> We journey out of hiddenness, to help others find holiness.

But if God must repeatedly convince each generation of their worth, power, ability and holiness, then we will continue treading upon a mountain that bears the trenches of left-over doubt from previous generations. This should not be! We owe it to the next generation to seek holiness and walk in boldness; they should not have to repeat what we had an opportunity to repeal.

Let's imagine for the moment a bride fully confident in her identity. It reminds me of Song of Solomon 4:7: 'You are altogether beautiful, my darling; there is no flaw in you.' A confident bride knows she is accepted, wanted and viewed through the lens of love. She is confident in her husband's love for her;

therefore she can trust her vulnerability within the walls of that protection. His security frees her to lower her defences, allowing her husband to know her intimately and explore her closely. Only a foundation of trust will permit this deep level of openness and sharing to unfold. As it is in personal relationships, so it is spiritually.

In the Old Testament we see numerous kings and judges who used their power for selfish gain, resulting in generations who lacked faith, and therefore lacked power. Moses was the antithesis of this – demonstrating faith through obedience and obtaining power through intimacy. Therefore, Joshua learned to stay in God's presence to gain power and stay in the word[3] to grow faith. His was the generation that saw the (Jericho) wall fall, the promise obtained and the future unveiled. Moses trusted the Lord, but it was Joshua who stayed in the tent (presence of God) long after Moses had left.

Our love relationship is here to create more than just goosebumps and nice feelings; it is here to create legacy. The King is coming back for a Bride who is ready, who knows her authority and who is walking in her identity. We must go from 'glory to glory' by seeking him with all of our heart, soul, mind and strength. It means putting him above our selfish desires and trusting him with our greatest dreams. When we say 'Yes, Lord' we open the door to new adventure and sign up to a life lived beyond our own comfort.

How Vulnerable Are You?

I was shocked. Using an online thesaurus, I entered the word 'vulnerability', anticipating a plethora of positive words I could choose from to continue my writing. What I didn't expect was page after page after page of words with *negative* connotations to them. I knew that one (or two) definitions of the word would be more negative, such as 'vulnerable to attack' or to 'disease', but to have so many words tinged with negativity? That surprised me. If we equate vulnerability with negativity, then it's no wonder we as a society don't want to become vulnerable with God!

> If we equate vulnerability with negativity, then it's no wonder we as a society don't want to become vulnerable with God!

Moses began his days refusing to be seen by the holy one, but he ended his days face to face: nothing hidden, embracing holiness, engulfed in glory. As we take responsibility and face our fears, confronting our disappointments and stepping out of hiddenness, we allow our lives to set an example for the next generation of being 'holy as he is holy', as seen in Leviticus 11:45: 'I am the LORD, who brought you up out of Egypt to be your God; therefore be holy, because I am holy.'

The Lord commanded it of his people in the Old Testament, and Peter reminded us of it in the New Testament:

> Therefore gird up the loins of your mind, be sober, and rest your hope fully upon the grace that is to be brought to you at the revelation of Jesus Christ; as obedient children, not conforming yourselves to the former lusts, as in your ignorance; but as He who called you is holy, you also be holy in all your conduct, because it is written, 'Be holy, for I am holy.'[4]

Holiness is not reserved for Sundays, communion or when the pastor is visiting. It is an exciting, beautiful lifestyle, which we alone can choose to live out. As we saw in chapter one, perfection is never meant to be our aim; otherwise our aim will soon become our master.

If we look further into the Greek word for 'perfect', used in Matthew 5:48 by Jesus, we will see it is the word *téleios*, meaning mature and fully developed, not flawlessly perfect.[5] We are being perfected as we walk in obedience to the perfect one – God the Father, through the Son and empowered by Holy Spirit. As we endeavour to obey his commandments (which, admittedly, is both a joy and a challenge!) we will automatically become more Christlike in our thoughts, behaviours and decisions . . . therefore, becoming more perfect with each step towards maturity in Christ.

But, as with everything, it is still a choice we must make – nobody ever stumbled into holiness.

> Nobody ever stumbled into holiness.

As for Me and My House

One of the best-known verses in the Old Testament is found in Joshua 24:15 where Joshua declares: 'But if serving the LORD seems undesirable to you, then choose for yourselves this day whom you will serve . . . as for me and my household, we will serve the Lord.'

The seeds of legacy left by Moses grew a harvest of righteousness lived by Joshua. Frequently, Moses needed to choose holiness when the circumstances tempted him to opt for easier options, such as leaving the Israelites to reap the consequences of their sin.[6] Joshua repeatedly saw Moses follow the Lord, forgive the people, seek righteousness and walk in justice. Choosing to draw near the Lord, instead of pulling back in times of difficulty, is a sign of a healthy love relationship. God is trustworthy and he is unchanging; he is a safe harbour and strong tower. There is no fear or condemnation in his love and he offers complete acceptance, even at our worst of times and behaviour. Any bride would be drawn to this kind of love!

Once we have a healthy picture of God's love individually, we can share that love corporately through the way we treat our neighbours, spouse, children and communities. Imagine the 'love revival' that could take place if we walked in our secure identities in Christ to such a level that our lives were never primarily about us, but about those seeking a love we had already found.

For Moses, being accepted by the Israelites was a concern early on, but as time went on it soon faded behind the glory of God's grace, goodness and compassion for all his children. Moses was secure because he took a risk, made new choices and remained humble.

Last year at this time I had just moved to a new city and I was praying about launching the ministry to a new level, as my sole vocation and income, living 100% by faith. To say I was nervous would be like saying the North Pole might be a tad chilly.

Up to this point I had always served another person's ministry (with pleasure) while doing some speaking or writing on the side. I had a calling and a dream, but I trusted the Lord's timing. In all honesty, I wasn't sure I wanted to move any further outside my comfort zone because what was once unknown had now become familiar. It has taken fifteen years but, in many ways, England is now more familiar to me than America. I imagine it's like getting married or having children – the unfamiliar and unknown at the beginning eventually becomes your safe place of being fully known. Perhaps that is why we need to continue having 'date nights' with our spouse or going on adventures with our kids . . . in order to stave off the inevitable lethargy that comes with comfort. Pyjamas are comfortable, but you aren't meant to live in them.

Anyway, one of the ventures I felt God put on my heart was what I decided to call 'Coffee with Jen'. It is a mentoring/coaching programme where I come alongside individuals to help them grow in their Christian faith – a bit like a 'faith coach'.[7] Something that has been highlighted to me through these sessions is that one person cannot make decisions for another. That has to be one of my most difficult challenges! I cannot choose to have faith-giving thoughts for someone else, or choose forgiveness for them, or speak life and not death over their circumstances . . . that is down to the individual and the Lord.

It is like a parent with their children. Often the wisest move a parent can make is allowing their child to learn for themselves, because trying to control them actually disempowers them, keeping them immature and dependent. If they are dependent, they are not free. A healthy parent creates safety for their child; a loving husband brings out beauty in his bride; and a kingdom-minded church leaves legacy for future generations.

The Bride of Christ is being prepared and we are part of that preparation. It has been quite a journey – from hiding in a basket to holiness on a mountain – and, as Moses' time draws to a close, we have one more opportunity to remind ourselves of the bigger picture and the role we play.

For Reflection

- 'Faith was never meant to set its borders around our dreams alone; it was designed to unlock the dreams of others.' How are you leaving a spiritual legacy for those following you?

- Does the word 'vulnerable' carry positive or negative connotations for you?

- If 'nobody ever stumbled into holiness', what would it look like for you to be more intentional in this area?

- Are you enabling anyone by making choices for them which they should be making themselves?

22

The Bride

Let us rejoice and be glad and give him glory!
For the wedding of the Lamb has come, and his
bride has made herself ready. Fine linen, bright
and clean, was given her to wear.

Rev. 19:7–9

As many young girls have done, I remember being a little girl putting a cloth on my head as my pretend 'veil' and walking down the imaginary aisle towards my beloved. As time went on and I got a bit older I can remember riding the school bus, staring out the window and dreaming of my future: I decided that I would stay single until I was 25 years old, at which time I would get married and we would begin a family at the age of 28. We would have two children, three at the most. It all seemed perfect and it never – ever – occurred to me that it might not happen as I had planned.

As a teenager I spent numerous hours dreaming of being pursued, wooed, wanted and cherished. I imagined myself and my husband laughing, dreaming, loving, and changing the world together. I was his favourite person and he was mine – it was safety personified.

Fast-forward about fifteen years, at which time I am in my early thirties watching all my friends date, get married and have children . . . leaving me standing alone at the imaginary 'starting line' of life.

As I write, I am approaching 50, and my friends' children are off to university and entering serious dating relationships themselves. Here I find myself . . . still waiting.

In my book *The Power of a Promise*[1] I share some of my testimony about singleness – waiting over the years for something to change and the gut-wrenching pain of not having children. It has been the most faith-challenging journey of my life, and as I've already said, I may never fully understand why that has been my particular road to navigate.

And yet, I know that throughout the years of wondering, waiting, watching and weeping, I discovered a love that no man will ever be able to give me. It is a love that runs deeper than touch and soothes greater than words. There are moments of ecstasy in the spirit, where it feels like you will explode if the glory gets any thicker. Times when heaven touches earth and the veil is remarkably thin, his love pouring through like liquid gold.

I know there are people who have actually gone to heaven (and come back to earth), encountering the glory of God in a way I have yet to experience. Others have known the Lord much longer than me and have stories I have yet to tell. I would never be so presumptuous as to think I am an expert or have mastered intimacy with the Lord.

But there is one thing I have learned: human love, while a stunning gift from God, cannot meet our deepest need. That is reserved for God – and God alone.

> But there is one thing I have learned: human love, while a stunning gift from God, cannot meet our deepest need. That is reserved for God – and God alone.

What Drives You?

In all transparency, I was driven to the Lord through my loneliness and pain more than my love and passion. Of course I loved him, but in reality, I needed him. My heart was breaking, and when that happens we usually either push towards the Lord or pull back from him. I was aware that he could 'solve my problem' at any time (find me a husband), but I also wanted his best for me and I knew that *he* wanted his best for me; sometimes his best simply doesn't make sense to our understanding. I made a choice to be OK with that, and the contentment that has followed is what I believe Paul means when he says there is a 'peace beyond understanding'.[2]

Years ago someone said to me: 'Jen, maybe the Lord is simply jealous for you and wants you all to himself?'

Gee, thanks.

I knew she meant well, but the last thing I wanted to hear in my late twenties was that I was never going to get married because God couldn't handle his jealousy. (I don't believe that was true, by the way.) God *is* jealous for us, but he also created love to fulfil us – both in heaven and on earth.

I was driven towards intimacy through loneliness and brokenness; Moses was driven towards intimacy through difficulty and challenge. This journey from hiddenness to holiness will take different paths for each one of us, and be led by different experiences and motives because this is a personal relationship with the Lord; there will literally *never* be another person in all of eternity who has your special, intimate relationship with him. To think otherwise is to limit God to a lack of creativity. If no two snowflakes are alike, then surely we each have our own eternal, personal, powerful walk with the Lord – growing in intensity to the degree we hunger for the King of kings and Lord of lords.

C.S. Lewis says: 'If God had no use for all these differences [among people], I do not see why He should have created more souls than one . . . your place in heaven will seem to be made for you and you alone because you were made for it.'[3]

There is a unique eternal home, for each unique eternal person, to enjoy our unique eternal love relationship. Let's press in to the uniqueness here and now, in this lifetime, discovering 'the one our soul loves' (see Song 3:4). It is there that innocence is restored and love, as it was meant to be from the beginning of time, can begin to flourish.

In chapter one, I shared how I thought my innocence was lost when the door of abuse slammed reality in my face. But I have learned that the depth of love, trust and vulnerability found in a holy place with God reopens a new door – one that contains a love no person, enemy or circumstance can touch or take away.

The Foreshadowing

What began with the Abrahamic covenant continues in the New Testament through Jesus and will be completely fulfilled when Revelation 7:9–10 becomes reality:

> After this I looked, and there before me was a great multitude that no one could count, from every nation, tribe, people and language, standing before the throne and before the Lamb. They were wearing white robes and were holding palm branches in their hands. And they cried out in a loud voice: 'Salvation belongs to our God, who sits on the throne, and to the Lamb.'

At that moment there will be no barriers, divisions, fear or shame, but only perfect love and astounding beauty – the Bridegroom

with his Bride in true vulnerability, intimacy and a union untouched for eternity.
Our intimacy with the Lord today is a fore-
shadowing of a much greater intimacy yet
to come. We are one person in a myriad
of millions worshipping our King; our unbridled vulnerability and transparency on

> Our intimacy with
> the Lord today is
> a foreshadowing
> of a much greater
> intimacy yet to
> come.

earth is a beautiful preparation for what is yet to come. The Bible
says we know in part, but there will come a time when we are
fully known. At that moment we will move from friend of God
to Bride of Christ:

> For we know in part and we prophesy in part, but when com-
> pleteness comes, what is in part disappears. When I was a child, I
> talked like a child, I thought like a child, I reasoned like a child.
> When I became a man, I put the ways of childhood behind me.
> For now we see only a reflection as in a mirror; then we shall see
> face to face. Now I know in part; then I shall know fully, even as
> I am fully known.[4]

Commentators say that Paul was probably referring to a mirror as known in that time, which would have been a type of
polished metal. It would never give a good reflection of reality,
so an imperfect view required a face-to-face meeting to see the
real. This is what we shall find in heaven.

When someone becomes a bride, she does not stop being
a friend; she moves her friendship to a deeper level of understanding and commitment. Heaven is the climax of all perfection, beauty and intimacy, coming together in an explosion of
worship to our King and Lord. What a thought!

Sometimes I sit and imagine heaven, reminding myself that
it is a very real place – pure joy, unrestricted freedom and peace

that is beyond earthly description. There will be colours we have not seen and sounds we have not heard; a reunion of saints and an understanding of the ages. Our Father presides over all and his love flows from the heavenly throne to swallow up every square inch of a kingdom overflowing with gold, jewels, beauty, freedom, laughter, prosperity and so much more. There is no room for sorrow or tears – they will never be experienced again!

Even Isaiah prophesied about a future marriage, hundreds of years before Jesus: 'I will greatly rejoice in the Lord, my soul shall exult in my God; for He has clothed me with the garments of salvation, He has covered me with the robe of righteousness, as a bridegroom decks himself with a garland, and as a bride adorns herself with her jewels.'[5]

> We are a bride meant to be seen, unveiled in beauty, enraptured by our bridegroom. He is not to be feared, but to be sought after – desired – spirit to spirit and heart to heart.

We are a bride meant to be seen, unveiled in beauty, enraptured by our bridegroom. He is not to be feared, but to be sought after – desired – spirit to spirit and heart to heart.

The Dance

Now Moses used to take a tent and pitch it outside the camp some distance away, calling it the 'tent of meeting'. Anyone enquiring of the Lord would go to the tent of meeting outside the camp. And whenever Moses went out to the tent, all the people rose and stood at the entrances to their tents, watching Moses until he entered the tent. As Moses went into the tent, the pillar of cloud would come down and stay at the entrance, while the Lord spoke with Moses. Whenever the people saw the pillar of cloud standing at the entrance to the tent, they all stood and worshipped, each at the entrance to their tent. The LORD would speak to Moses face to face, as one speaks to a friend. Then Moses would return to the camp, but his young assistant Joshua son of Nun did not leave the tent.[6]

I love so many aspects of these verses that I want to finish by revisiting them. Numbers 12:8 says that God spoke with Moses 'mouth to mouth', which appears even more intimate than face to face. The Divine desires a closeness that transcends distance, and an intimacy that overcomes insecurity. He comes as close as we will allow and whispers truths as deep as we can receive. He will never force himself into our space, nor will he reject us when we seek his.

> A God in heaven is stretching out his hand, eyes dancing with the light of love, heart filled with expectation and desire, saying to you: 'May I have this dance?'

I imagine it is like a beautiful, intimate dance. A God in heaven is stretching out his hand, eyes dancing with the light of love, heart filled with expectation and desire, saying to you: 'May I have this dance?'

His invitation creates a new rhythm of love. One that depends not on rules and regulations, but on trust and acceptance. It is a dance forged in the flames of challenge and fuelled by the strength of faith. This dance lets him fully lead – gracefully moving us around the room of our next season – causing our heart to beat with expectation and excitement, tempting the edge of unease, yet resting on the side of safety.

We move with such beauty, intensity and power that the peace we feel nearly sweeps us off our feet – is it possible to maintain this much contentment and joy, regardless of life's circumstances?

Can I trust him to maintain a tight grip, as he lifts me off the floor of security and into the air of the unknown?

Trying to surrender, I hear him whisper 'Relax' . . . and with that I allow my fear to be swallowed up in a love that I had only once dreamed of: one I thought originated from earth, yet now I know is released from heaven.

Song of Solomon 2:10–13 says:

My beloved speaks and says to me:
'Arise, my love, my beautiful one,
    and come away,
for behold, the winter is past;
    the rain is over and gone.
The flowers appear on the earth,
    the time of singing has come,
and the voice of the turtle-dove
    is heard in our land.
The fig tree ripens its figs,
    and the vines are in blossom;
    they give forth fragrance.
Arise, my love, my beautiful one,
    and come away.'

The bush is burning . . . the mountain is calling . . . his invitation is waiting . . . it's time.

Will you step out of hiddenness and trust his holiness?
Face.
To.
Face.

For Reflection

- If Moses was driven to the Lord through difficulty and challenge, what has drawn (or draws) you to a deeper place with the Lord?

- In what way is your relationship with God today preparing you for eternity with him as part of the Bride of Christ?

- What have you learned on this journey and how has it brought you into a more face-to-face relationship with God?

- In your own way, spend time revelling in God's love for you and your love for him: face to face.

A Prayer for My Bridegroom

From my first breath until our first embrace . . . thank you for desiring and pursuing me.

For so long I have wanted to know you more, yet fear has kept me from giving you more – uncertain of your response to my humanity. Would you want the unedited, uncovered nakedness of my heart? Now, I believe that you do.

I am ready to trust – and risk – again; to experience your unrelenting love as I unveil and share the deepest (and most hidden) parts of my soul with you.

My ultimate desire is knowing more of you: experiencing deeper layers of your affection, touching greater levels of your peace, tasting every drop of your amazing grace.

Shame is no longer my identity and hiding is no longer my friend.

It is you that I want,

as my best friend, my safe harbour and my truest love.

I am yours . . . and I will love you from now into eternity.

Your Bride

Author's Note

Thank you for sharing this journey of intimacy with me! I pray that you have been encouraged, challenged and inspired for the exciting future ahead. God loves you deeply and uniquely – nobody will ever have your calling (God's plan for your life) or your relationship with the Lord.

The greatest decision we could ever make in life is to follow the Lord wholeheartedly. Trusting him with our future takes courage, yet he has promised never to leave us and never to forsake us (Heb. 13:5). If you would like to become a Christian, or re-dedicate your life to Christ, please pray the following prayer with me:

Dear God,

I come to you in the name of Jesus. I admit that I have not trusted you to be my Saviour and have tried to live on my own terms. I ask you to forgive me of all my sins. The Bible says if I confess with my mouth that 'Jesus is Lord', and believe in my heart that God raised him from the dead, I will be saved (Rom. 10:9). I believe with my heart and I confess with my mouth that Jesus is the Lord and Saviour of my life from this moment forward. Thank you for saving me!

In Jesus' name I pray. Amen.

If you have prayed that prayer, I would love to celebrate with you! Please let me know by emailing your testimony to jen@jenbaker.co.uk. Also, please share with a trusted friend and find a strong Bible-teaching, Spirit-filled church to become part of, as we cannot do this journey alone.

Finally, I would love to stay in touch with you through social media. You can find me on Instagram, Facebook and Twitter here: @jenbakerinspire

Notes

Introduction

1 L.B. Cowman, *Streams in the Desert* (Grand Rapids, MI: Zondervan, 1997), p. 83.

1: The Garden

1 US English: apartment.
2 US English: parking lot.
3 Ezek. 28:12.
4 1 Cor. 13:9–13 ESV (emphasis mine).
5 Paula Gooder, 'On Being (Im)perfect', *Paula Gooder*, blog (5 Sept. 2016) https://www.gooder.me.uk/on-being-imperfect/.
6 Harold W. Perkins, *The Doctrine of Christian or Evangelical Perfection* (London: Epworth Press, 1927), pp. 52–3 (italics in the original); cited in the Discovery Bible notes on the Greek word for 'perfect' (Strong's G5046) https://thediscoverybible.com.
7 Sonship includes both male and female.
8 Gen. 1:28–30.

2: The Gamble

[1] John 2:23–24.
[2] John Bevere, 'The Weapon of Grace', *Messenger International* https://messengerinternational.org/blog/devotional/weapon-grace-2 (accessed 15 Nov. 2018).

3: The Gap

[1] Heb. 11:24–25.
[2] Quoted in Mark Ballenger, 'What Does the Bible Say about Blind Spots?', *Apply God's Word* (2017).
[3] 2 Sam. 12.

4: I Was Born This Way

[1] Matt. 7:3–5.
[2] Celia Walden, 'We Take One Million Selfies Every Day – But What Are They Doing to Our Brains?' *The Telegraph* (2016). https://www.telegraph.co.uk/women/life/we-take-1-million-selfies-every-day---but-what-are-they-doing-to/.
[3] Neil T. Anderson, *Victory Over the Darkness* (Ventura, CA: Regal, 2000), p. 47.
[4] Michal E. Hunt, 'Moses' Childhood and Early Life in Egypt and Midian', *Agape Bible Study* (2009) https://www.AgapeBible Study.com/Exodus/Exodus_Lesson_2.htm (accessed 23 Nov. 2018).
[5] Rabbi Ken Spiro, 'History Crash Course #9', *Aish.com* (2000) http://www.aish.com/jl/h/cc/48931697.html.
[6] YMCA, *In Your Face* (2018) https://www.ymca.org.uk/wp-content/uploads/2018/02/In-Your-Face-Executive-Summary.pdf.

5: The Disconnect

1   See Mic. 6:8.
2   Rom. 12:21.
3   Exod. 2:16–22.

6: Love Hurts

1   Vid Buggs Jr, 'Inspiring Quotes by Mother Teresa on Kindness, Love and Charity', quote 1, *Everyday Power* https://everydaypowerblog .com/quotes-by-mother-teresa/.
2   Vid Buggs Jr, 'Inspiring Quotes by Mother Teresa on Kindness, Love and Charity', quote 19, *Everyday Power* https://everyday-powerblog.com/quotes-by-mother-teresa/.
3   Joyce Meyer, *The Root of Rejection* (Tulsa, OK: Harrison House, 1994), p. 44.

7: How Do I Get Out?

1   Quote taken from DECISION magazine, March 2013; "Praying in Faith" part 3, by Jerry Bridges. ©2013 Billy Graham Evangelistic Association. Used by permission, all rights reserved. https:// billygraham.org/decision-magazine/march-2013/praying-in-faith/.
2   John Bevere, 'How Complaining Halts Your Destiny', *Charisma* (2013) https://www.charismamag.com/spirit/spiritual-growth/ 17508-john-bevere-how-complaining-halts-your-destiny.

8: Make It Personal

1   US English: chat.
2   HELPS Word-studies taken from The Discovery Bible software, available at thediscoverybible.com, copyright © 2018, HELPS Ministries Inc. Used by permission. All rights reserved.

3   HELPS Word-studies taken from The Discovery Bible software, available at thediscoverybible.com, copyright © 2018, HELPS Ministries Inc. Used by permission. All rights reserved.
4   Matt. 3:17.
5   Jas 4:8.

9: What a Difference a Day Makes

1   Member of Parliament.
2   Exod. 3:1–10 (emphasis mine).
3   Marcus Jastrow et al., 'Burning Bush', *Jewish Encyclopedia* (originally published 1906) http://www.jewishencyclopedia.com/articles/3845-burning-bush.
4   Taking into account the whole of the story, many theologians presume this is Jesus, the Second Person of the Trinity, appearing prior to his birth.

10: Resistance and Roadblocks

1   US English: dollars.
2   Donald Miller, '5 Ways to Make Your Customer the Hero in Your Marketing Material', *Building a StoryBrand* http://buildingastorybrand.com/customer-the-hero-in-marketing-material.
3   Acts 7:35.
4   Jer. 17:9.

11: The Reward of Risk

1   See John 10:10 AMPC.
2   HELPS Word-studies taken from *The Discovery Bible* software, available at thediscoverybible.com, copyright © 2018, HELPS Ministries Inc. Used by permission. All rights reserved.

3   Rom. 2:4.
4   Jas 4:7.
5   One of the names of God, meaning Provider.

12: In Battle

1   https://www.goodreads.com/quotes/721301-fear-is-a-reaction-
    courage-is-a-decision.
2   Num. 20:11–12.

13: No Way Out

1   Andrew Murray, *The Holiest of All* (Fort Worth, TX: Kenneth
    Copeland Ministries, abridged edn, 1993), p. 482.
2   Read 2 Kgs 6:14–23 for a good example of this.

14: Through the Wilderness

1   Exod. 15:22–24.
2   Exod. 15:25–27.
3   See John 17:4 MSG.
4   'Children Feel Safer with Boundaries', *Preaching Today* (2018)
    https://www.preachingtoday.com/illustrations/2018/march/
    children-feel-safer-with-boundaries.html.
5   Jen Baker, *The Power of a Promise* (Milton Keynes: Authentic
    Media, 2018).

15: On the Mountain

1   Not his real name.
2   Exod. 20:18–21 (emphasis mine).

3   Deut. 5:5.
4   EU Kids Online, *Findings, Methods, Recommendations* (2014); UK Safer Internet Centre. *Friendship in a Digital Age* (2015); cited in Action for Children, *It Starts with Hello: A Report Looking into the Impact of Loneliness in Children, Young People and Families* (2017) https://www.actionforchildren.org.uk/media/9724/action_for_children_it_starts_with_hello_report__november_2017_lowres.pdf.
5   Sean Coughlin, 'Loneliness More Likely to Affect Young People', *BBC News* (2018) https://www.bbc.co.uk/news/education-43711606.
6   'The Human Brain is Loaded Daily with 34 GB of Information', *Tech 21 Century* https://www.tech21century.com/the-human-brain-is-loaded-daily-with-34-gb-of-information/.
7   HM Government, Department for Digital, Culture, Media and Sport, *A Connected Society: A Strategy for Tackling Loneliness – Laying the Foundations for Change* (2018) https://assets.publishing.service.gov.uk/government/uploads/system/uploads/attachment_data/file/750909/6.4882_DCMS_Loneliness_Strategy_web_Update.pdf.
8   See Exod. 20:21.
9   Exod. 32:1.
10 https://biblehub.com/commentaries/mhc/exodus/32.htm.
11 Num. 12:3.
12 Ps. 62:6 TPT.

16: Living Intentionally

1   Exegetical commentary on Luke 2:52 from Cambridge Bible for Schools and Colleges https://biblehub.com/commentaries/luke/2-52.htm.
2   https://www.goodreads.com/quotes/978-whether-you-think-you-can-or-you-think-you-can-t--you-re.
3   Jentzen Franklin, *Fasting: Opening the Door to a Deeper, More Intimate, More Powerful Relationship with God* (Lake Mary, FL: Charisma House, 2008).

4   Franklin, *Fasting*, p. 84.
5   Andrew Murray, *The Holiest of All* (Fort Worth, TX: Kenneth Copeland Ministries, abridged edn, 1993), p. 136.
6   https://www.goodreads.com/quotes/578503-before-you-criticize-a-man-walk-a-mile-in-his.

17: The Big Questions

1   Martin B. Copenhaver, *Jesus Is the Question: The 307 Questions Jesus Asked and the 3 He Answered* (Nashville, TN: Abingdon Press, 2014) https://www.amazon.co.uk/Jesus-Question-Questions-Asked-Answered/dp/1426755147.
2   Gal. 4:6.
3   Job 40:4.
4   Matt. 5:6 AMPC.

18: Glory

1   *The Discovery Bible* software is available at thediscoverybible.com.
2   Alexander MacLaren, *MacLaren's Commentary: Expositions of Holy Scripture* taken from *The Discovery Bible* software, available at the-discoverybible.com, copyright © 2018, HELPS Ministries Inc. Used by permission. All rights reserved.
3   1 Cor. 15:41–54.
4   Voice message from Dr Gary Hill who was awarded an honorary doctoral degree (LittD, 1990) in recognition of his work in biblical Hebrew and Greek, embodied in the best-selling study Bible, *The Discovery Bible New Testament* (ed. Gleason L. Archer; Chicago, IL: Moody Press, 1987).
5   Gen. 1:2.
6   Exod. 33:19–20.

19: The Clue Is in the Cleft

[1] HELPS Word-studies taken from *The Discovery Bible* software, available at thediscoverybible.com, copyright © 2018, HELPS Ministries Inc. Used by permission. All rights reserved.

[2] Lisa Bevere, *Adamant: Finding Truth in a Universe of Opinions* (Grand Rapids, MI: Revell, 2018), p. 18.

[3] Exod. 32.

20: The Cloud

[1] Ps. 139:13–16.

[2] UK English: university.

[3] Quoted in Tom Ziglar, 'If You Aim at Nothing . . .', *Ziglar* https://www.ziglar.com/articles/if-you-aim-at-nothing-2/.

[4] US English: checkout.

[5] https://www.goodreads.com/quotes/979454-the-bible-is-not-only-a-book-which-was-once.

[6] Rachel Held Evans, *A Year of Biblical Womanhood: How a Liberated Woman Found Herself Sitting on Her Roof, Covering Her Head, and Calling Her Husband 'Master'* (Nashville, TN: Thomas Nelson, 2012), p. 188.

21: The Next Generation

[1] Used with permission.

[2] Andrew Murray, *The Holiest of All* (Fort Worth, TX: Kenneth Copeland Ministries, abridged edn, 1993), pp. 486–7.

[3] Josh. 1:8.

[4] 1 Pet. 1:13–16 NKJV.

5   HELPS Word-studies taken from *The Discovery Bible* software, available at thediscoverybible.com, copyright © 2018, HELPS Ministries Inc. Used by permission. All rights reserved.

6   Exod. 32:9–10.

7   https://www.jenbaker.co.uk/coffee-with-jen.

22: The Bride

1   Jen Baker, *The Power of a Promise* (Milton Keynes: Authentic Media, 2018).

2   See Phil. 4:7.

3   THE PROBLEM OF PAIN by CS Lewis © copyright CS Lewis Pte Ltd 1940 (New York, NY: HarperCollins, 1996), p. 147; cited in the Discovery Bible notes on Strong's #110 https://thediscoverybible.com.

4   1 Cor. 13:9–12.

5   Isa. 61:10 AMPC.

6   Exod. 33:7–11.

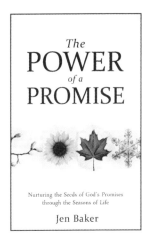

The Power of a Promise

Nurturing the seeds of God's promises through the seasons of life

Jen Baker

God loves to sow promises in our hearts, but they very rarely come to fruition immediately. Too often the storms of life can rob us of our hope, and we can give up on these promises. But what if these dark times were all part of the journey to fulfilled promises – would that give us hope to persevere?

Using a seed as a metaphor for the journey, Jen Baker shares six key stages a promise undergoes on its way to fulfilled purpose. Each stage of the journey is detailed, including what to expect and how we could respond.

Weaving together biblical reflections and real-life experiences, Jen inspires us to look at how we can all live fully in the calling God has uniquely designed for each of us.

978-1-78078-986-6

Finding Our Voice

*Unsung lives from the Bible
resonating with stories from today*

Jeannie Kendall

The Bible is full of stories of people facing issues that are
still surprisingly relevant today. Within its pages, people have
wrestled with problems such as living with depression, losing a
child, overcoming shame, and searching for meaning. Yet these
are not always the stories of the well-known heroes of faith, but
those of people whose names are not even recorded.

Jeannie Kendall brings these unnamed people to vibrant life.
Their experiences are then mirrored by a relevant testimony
from someone dealing with a similar situation today.

Finding Our Voice masterfully connects the past with the
present day, encouraging us to identify with the characters'
stories, and giving us hope that, whatever the circumstances,
we are all 'known to God'.

978-1-78893-037-6

Infused with Life

*Exploring God's gift of rest in
a world of busyness*

Andy Percey

In a stressful, task-orientated life, we know the importance of
rest, but it is too often pushed out of our busy schedules.

Join Andy Percey as he reveals that rest is actually God's good
gift to us, provided for us to experience a balance in our lives
that isn't just about rest as recovery, but rest as harmony with
our Creator and the world he has made.

By learning to practise life-giving rhythms of rest, we can be
infused with the very best of the life God freely gives us.

978-1-78893-065-9

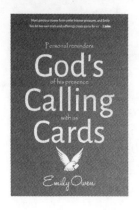

God's Calling Cards

*Personal reminders of his
presence with us*

Emily Owen

What does it mean to be called – or to hear the call of God?

Using biblical examples and moving personal testimony, Emily
Owen invites us to lean in to listen to God, to expect him to
speak and, ultimately, to be close enough to hear and recognize
his voice.

This devotional gently encourages us to personally encounter
the God who loves us and to look out for God's calling cards in
our lives.

978-1-78893-025-3

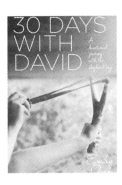

30 Days with David
A devotional journey with the
shepherd boy
Emily Owen
978-1-78078-449-6
978-1-78078-451-9 (e-book)

30 Days with John
A devotional journey with the
disciple
Emily Owen
978-1-86024-936-5
978-1-78078-257-7 (e-book)

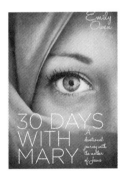

30 Days with Mary
A devotional journey with the
mother of Jesus
Emily Owen
978-1-86024-935-8
978-1-78078-255-3 (e-book)

30 Days with Elijah
A devotional journey with the
prophet
Emily Owen
978-1-86024-937-2
978-1-78078-256-0 (e-book)

Authentic

We trust you enjoyed reading this book from Authentic. If you want to be informed of any new titles from this author and other releases you can sign up to the Authentic newsletter by scanning below:

Online:
authenticmedia.co.uk

Follow us: